C000268753

65 FARMERS' MARKET
ORGANIC SEASONAL RECIPES

65 FARMERS' MARKET
ORGANIC SEASONAL RECIPES

Making the most of fresh, wholesome and healthy produce in a delicious
range of easy everyday recipes, shown step by step in 280 photographs

YSANNE SPEVACK

HERMES
HOUSE

This edition is published by Hermes House
an imprint of Anness Publishing Ltd
Hermes House, 88–89 Blackfriars Road, London SE1 8HA
tel. 020 7401 2077; fax 020 7633 9499

www.hermeshouse.com; www.annesspublishing.com

If you like the images in this book and would like to investigate
using them for publishing, promotions or advertising, please visit
our website www.practicalpictures.com for more information.

Publisher: Joanna Lorenz
Editorial Director: Helen Sudell
Editors: Joy Wotton, Elizabeth Woodland, Simona Hill
Jacket Design: Nigel Partridge
Photographers: Peter Anderson and Simon Smith
Production Controller: Bessie Bai

ETHICAL TRADING POLICY
Because of our ongoing ecological investment programme, you,
as our customer, can have the pleasure and reassurance of
knowing that a tree is being cultivated on your behalf to naturally
replace the materials used to make the book you are holding.
For further information, go to www.annesspublishing.com/trees

© Anness Publishing Ltd 2011

All rights reserved. No part of this publication may be
reproduced, stored in a retrieval system, or transmitted in any
way or by any means, electronic, mechanical, photocopying,
recording or otherwise, without the prior written permission of
the copyright holder.

A CIP catalogue record for this book is available from
the British Library.

Previously published as part of a larger volume,
The Farmer's Market Cookbook

NOTES
Bracketed terms are intended for American readers.
For all recipes, quantities are given in both metric and imperial
measures and, where appropriate, in standard cups and spoons.
Follow one set of measures, but not a mixture, because they are
not interchangeable.
Standard spoon and cup measures are level. 1 tsp = 5ml,
1 tbsp = 15ml, 1 cup = 250ml/8fl oz.
Australian standard tablespoons are 20ml. Australian readers
should use 3 tsp in place of 1 tbsp for measuring small quantities.
American pints are 16fl oz/2 cups. American readers should use
20fl oz/2.5 cups in place of 1 pint when measuring liquids.
Electric oven temperatures in this book are for conventional
ovens. When using a fan oven, the temperature will probably
need to be reduced by about 10–20°C/20–40°F. Since ovens
vary, you should check with your manufacturer's instruction
book for guidance.
Medium (US large) eggs are used unless otherwise stated.

PUBLISHER'S NOTE
Although the advice and information in this book are believed to
be accurate and true at the time of going to press, neither the
authors nor the publisher can accept any legal responsibility or
liability for any errors or omissions that may have been made nor
for any inaccuracies nor for any loss, harm or injury that comes
about from following instructions or advice in this book.

CONTENTS

WHAT IS A FARMERS' MARKET?

Like a traditional market, a farmers' market is a place where people come to sell produce, usually in an open space central to a community. A farmers' market is not necessarily restricted to sales by farmers, but to all producers involved in creating food and drink usually within a specified radius of the market. Such markets operate according to a set of principles: all produce sold must be farmed, reared, baked, caught, brewed, pickled or smoked by the stallholder. Produce does not necessarily have to be organic. However, a feature of the market is that meat and poultry for sale have been reared in a humane way or allowed to grow naturally without recourse to artificial stimulants. As a result the emphasis is on high quality and taste, with freshness as well as value for money being top priorities. Such markets often offer local specialities too, helping to keep valuable traditions alive.

Supporting local farmers' markets helps the customer indirectly play an active role in maintaining the quality of the land. By choosing produce that is grown naturally or reared according to its natural instincts we are able to support the farmer in his work of keeping the land in good order.

Farmers' markets are gaining in popularity and are often a significant attraction. They benefit the local economy by helping to keep farmers and producers in business, and money paid for goods continues to circulate within the community sustaining employment for local people.

Buying Direct

There are many other benefits to farmers' markets, including the encouragement of small-scale businesses, each with specialist knowledge and a wealth of information to share. One key benefit of buying produce direct from the grower is to maintain a valid connection with our food. Purchasing items from the person who grew them, or who had a hand in nurturing the animal, allows information about the produce to be exchanged. A farmer might also welcome feedback on new varieties of crops that he is experimenting with, and customers can let him know which fruit or vegetables they have enjoyed. Best of all, in cutting out different stages of the sales process

Below: Fruit and vegetables on sale at a local farmers' market are picked when they are at their peak.

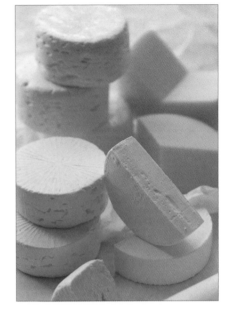

Above: Handmade cheese is often available at farmers' markets, and there may be the chance to test the produce before you make your purchase.

and by going direct to market, farmers can sell their produce when it is at its peak in terms of flavour. The shortened timeframe from harvesting to market means the nutrient value of fruit and vegetables is retained and its freshness preserved. In addition, food will generally have travelled fewer miles to get to market and will be sold with less packaging, both significant benefits to the environment. Farmers also get a much better deal selling their food direct to the customer, generally obtaining about double the price at a farmers' market than they would if they sold the produce to the supermarket.

Increased Nutrition

Locally grown food is more nutritious than food that has been flown in from another country. Fruit and vegetables for export are often picked before they are fully ripe and kept chilled to avoid spoilage, adding another cost. This means that they fail to develop the complex flavours and nutritional compounds available in produce that has been allowed to ripen naturally and that which has been freshly picked.

SEASONAL FOOD

Bursting with ingredients flown from all over the world, supermarkets present us with a vast array of produce that is quick, easy and convenient to buy. Although more of us are taking notice of the point-of-origin labels on our food, subconsciously clocking up the food miles it has travelled and wondering how fresh it really is, how many of us would be able to transform our culinary habits to eat what is naturally in season on a countrywide, if not local, basis? Yet seasonal food, with its associations of sustainability and supporting the local economy, has become the latest idea to receive positive marketing.

Taste and Flavour

Each season provides us with a vast array of edible produce that reaches its peak of flavour and abundance at a specific time of year. Nature provides us with a rich bounty of food, and when harvested and bought fresh, it is tastier and more nutritious than out-of-season food, which has leached its nutritional value on its journey to the supermarket. Fruit and vegetables that germinate naturally are stronger and provide better-quality produce that has more taste than any out-of-season food could hope to supply. Fresh crops

Above: Asparagus has a very short season in early summer. It is a treat to be savoured at its best.

manufactured to supply supermarkets with year-round deliveries are grown in artificial conditions and boosted with fertilizers. Such food cannot replicate the taste of naturally grown fresh produce in season. Strawberries in winter, for example, look fabulous but taste bland.

Above: Pumpkin and squash ripen in autumn, providing comforting and filling fare for the cooler months.

The Changing Year

Cooking with food that is seasonal helps us to connect to the rhythm of the changing year. Even if we do not make a conscious effort to buy seasonal foods, we still associate certain foods with the seasons as well as with specific celebrations, such as lamb in spring, strawberries in summer, and turkey for Christmas. Usually we want to eat heartier meals in winter, when it is cold, and lighter dishes in summer. Our natural inclinations to eat these foods has, in effect, been suppressed by the wide availability of supermarket produce.

When in season, food has reached its natural maturity, making it more flavourful, abundant and cheaper to buy. And if we choose to buy from local sources such as the farmers' market, we are helping to reduce the number of air miles that food travels to reach its destination, increasing the chances of it retaining nutritional value as well as supporting local producers and the local economy.

Left: Geese are in season in the early winter months. The meat tastes richer than the dark meat of turkey.

CHOOSING ORGANIC FOOD

Interest in organic food and farming is at an all-time high. This is partly because people are better informed about nutrition, more concerned about the environment and more cautious about the effects of diet on health than at any time in the past; but there are also more fundamental reasons, such as flavour. Everybody wants to eat food that tastes good, and so it is hardly surprising that people are choosing organic produce, which is widely regarded as having better flavour than that which has been produced in an artificial way.

Why Eat Organic Food?

There are sound reasons why organic food tastes better. The slower growth rates of organic crops allow more time for flavour and nutrients to develop naturally. A wholesome, organic diet provides balanced nutrition, including a healthy range of vitamins, minerals and phytonutrients.

Improved Immunity There is evidence to suggest that people who eat organic food build up a stronger immunity to disease than those who consistently eat food that is laden with chemicals.

Below: Livestock, such as sheep, raised on organic farms enjoy a healthier lifestyle.

Increased Fertility Studies appear to support a link between organic diets and increased fertility in men. Because a balanced organic diet is more nutritionally sound and contains fewer chemicals or artificial hormones than a non-organic diet, it is bound to offer the best option for men – and women – wanting to support their sexual health and improve their chances of conceiving.

Vitamins and Minerals The reason that fresh organic produce contains more vitamins and minerals than the agrochemical equivalent is largely due to the method of cultivation. Organic fruits and vegetables are not sprayed with artificial fertilizers, but are allowed to grow and ripen more naturally in richer soil, obtaining the maximum variety of micronutrients.

Phytonutrients All fresh produce contains these naturally occurring chemical compounds, but organic produce contains more than its non-organic equivalent. They help to fight disease and promote good health.

Fats Hydrogenated fats are oils that become solid or semi-solid at room temperature. Nutritionists agree that they are a major co-factor in heart disease, cancer, diabetes and obesity. The surest way to remove hydrogenated

fats from your diet is to go organic. Organic food regulations throughout the world prohibit the use of hydrogenated fats. Saturated fat is present in organic beef as well as in intensively reared beef, but the percentage is likely to be lower.

The Chemical Cocktail

The average adult living in one of the industrialized nations has between 300 and 500 agrochemical pesticides in his or her body at any one time. Pesticides can remain stored in body fat for many years. No long-term studies have truly evaluated the damage to our health these chemicals pose, but there is evidence to suggest they exacerbate chronic conditions and seriously undermine health.

Additives Alarmingly, 7,000 artificial additives are permitted to be used in conventional food. Only seven of these are allowed to be used in processed organic food.

Antibiotics and Hormones Intensively reared livestock are routinely fed and injected with antibiotics to keep them healthy. These substances pass into their meat. People who eat this meat develop reduced immunity through over-exposure to antibiotics.

What is Organic Food?

Food labelled organic has been produced according to strict and rigidly regulated guidelines. Organic farming is the cultivation of crops and rearing of livestock with natural soil fertility at the heart of the system. Organic farmers believe that by working to maintain and encourage good soil structure, the crops and livestock grown and bred there will flourish. The system of farming is socially and environmentally conscious. It seeks to promote natural biological cycles, encourage biological diversity and enrich the soil structure by natural means. The management practices that sustain such activity aim to reduce soil erosion; promote ecological harmony in the immediate and wider landscape; reduce fossil fuel consumption in the pursuit of good farming practice; and grow produce without the routine use of pesticides or artificial fertilizers.

Right: Organic produce is not just about the food we put on our plates, but is a philosophy for living that resonates deeply with many people. Organic diary products manufactured from animals that eat a natural, unadulterated diet do not contain harmful additives that will be passed into the human food chain.

Organic Crops
Fruit and vegetables that are grown organically are generally grown on a smaller scale than those that are non-organic. This is because organic farming is more labour intensive. Some vegetables require soil rich in specific nutrients, and if they are grown for too long on one plot of land it will be depleted of those nutrients. Other vegetables help to fix those same nutrients in the ground. It therefore makes sense to follow a system known as crop rotation. Vegetables belonging to one plant family are planted together in a plot of land. The same plot will be planted with a different vegetable family

Below: Box schemes offer an easy method of introducing organic produce into your diet, and best of all they deliver direct to your door or even workplace. They can be tailored to your specific needs.

the following year, and with a different vegetable family again the year after that. The crops thus rotate over several different plots, allowing the land to recover from each depletion.

This system also helps to curb the increase in soil-borne pests and diseases that thrive on a certain crop, since they may die out when their food source is removed and a less vulnerable plant takes its place over subsequent years.

Organic vegetables are grown to be deep rooting, which means that they draw nutrients from the subsoil, rather than being fed them with artificial means. The soil is replenished with green manures, crops which grow in the plot, and are then dug back into that soil once they have grown to maturity. Many green manures are available and each fixes different nutrients into the ground.

Organic Livestock Farming
Animal welfare is a fundamental principle of organic livestock, poultry and dairy farming. Animals and poultry from an organic farm are nurtured without recourse to antibiotics or routine drugs, and their diet is solvent-free. Organic farmers are not allowed to use hormones to encourage animal growth or increase milk production. All organically reared animals that are naturally herbivorous are fed only a

vegetarian diet. Organic meat and dairy produce is free from genetically modified organisms or GMOs because all food for organically reared animals must be GMO-free by law. Organically reared animals are always free range.

Organic Fish
Whether wild or farmed, organically reared fish should come from sustainable fisheries and farms and be caught using fishing practices that protect the environment.

Logic dictates that all wild fish are organic, since they swim and eat where they will. However, pollution, insensitive fishing methods and proximity to major shipping lanes all have a detrimental effect on fish stocks, and there is no standard for organics here.

The conditions under which fish are farmed vary widely. For farmed fish to be labelled organic they must have adequate room to move, be allowed to grow and develop naturally, and be given organic feed.

The range of organic foods may not be as great as that of non-organic produce, but the pleasure of enjoying seasonal treats such as strawberries in summer, at the same time as helping to sustain the environment provides a more than adequate compensation.

SPRING

As the days start to lengthen and the weather gets warmer, the fresh organic ingredients traditionally associated with this time of year – such as tender young vegetables and new season's lamb – start to appear in the shops and farmers' markets. This season's vegetables require little cooking to bring out their sweet flavour: try asparagus with a tangy lemon sauce, sweet young carrots and leeks, or escalopes of chicken with new potatoes. Brightly coloured spring vegetables also look and taste good when served with pasta, or when added to soups. Light fish dishes are a popular choice now after the long, dark winter days – Salmon Fish Cakes, served simply with spring vegetables, are a real treat. This is also the time of year to enjoy organic lamb, in dishes such as Herb-crusted Rack of Lamb with Puy Lentils, and Lamb Burgers with Red Onion and Tomato Relish. For dessert, nothing tastes better than tender spring rhubarb served with ginger ice cream.

PASTA and CHICKPEA SOUP

A simple, country-style soup that is easy to make and filling to eat. Many of these ingredients are store-cupboard staples. Look out for really large pasta shells, which you can find in farmers' markets and good organic stores.

SERVES FOUR TO SIX

1 onion
2 carrots
2 celery sticks
60ml/4 tbsp olive oil
400g/14oz can chickpeas, rinsed
    and drained
200g/7oz can cannellini beans,
    rinsed and drained
150ml/¼ pint/⅔ cup passata (bottled
    strained tomatoes)
120ml/4fl oz/½ cup water
1.5 litres/2½ pints/6¼ cups chicken stock
2 fresh or dried rosemary sprigs
200g/7oz dried giant conchiglie
sea salt and ground black pepper
freshly grated Parmesan cheese or
    premium Italian-style vegetarian
    cheese, to serve

1 Chop the onion, carrots and celery sticks finely, either in a food processor or by hand.

2 Heat the olive oil in a large pan, add the chopped vegetable mixture and cook over a low heat, stirring frequently, for 5 minutes, or until the vegetables are just beginning to soften.

3 Add the chickpeas and cannellini beans, stir well to mix, then cook for 5 minutes. Stir in the passata and water, then cook, stirring, for 2–3 minutes.

4 Add 475ml/16fl oz/2 cups of the stock and one of the rosemary sprigs. Bring to the boil, cover, then simmer gently, stirring occasionally, for 1 hour.

5 Pour in the remaining stock, add the pasta and bring to boil, stirring. Lower the heat slightly and simmer, stirring frequently, until the pasta is *al dente*: 7–8 minutes or according to the instructions on the packet.

6 When the pasta is cooked, taste the soup for seasoning. Remove the rosemary and serve the soup hot in warmed bowls, topped with grated cheese and a few rosemary leaves from the rosemary sprig.

COOK'S TIP
Organic passata is a must for this recipe as most non-organic tomato products contain genetically modified tomatoes.

CHICKEN, AVOCADO and SPRING ONION SOUP

Organic avocados ripen naturally over a longer period of time than non-organic ones, producing really rich-flavoured fruit. Buy them and store until ripe before use. Combined here with chicken and spring onions they add a creaminess to this delicious soup.

SERVES SIX

1.5 litres/2½ pints/6¼ cups chicken stock
½ fresh chilli, seeded
2 skinless, boneless chicken breast fillets
1 avocado
4 spring onions (scallions), finely sliced
400g/14oz can chickpeas, drained
sea salt and freshly ground black pepper

1 Pour the chicken stock into a large pan and add the chilli. Bring to the boil, add the whole chicken breast fillets, then lower the heat and simmer for about 10 minutes, or until the chicken is cooked.

COOK'S TIP
Handle chillies with care as they can irritate the skin and eyes. It is advisable to wear rubber gloves when preparing them.

2 Remove the pan from the heat and lift out the chicken breasts with a slotted spoon. Leave to cool a little, then, using two forks, shred the chicken into small pieces. Set the shredded chicken aside.

3 Pour the chicken stock into a food processor or blender and add the chilli. Process the mixture until smooth, then return to the pan.

4 Cut the avocado in half, remove the skin and stone (pit), then slice the flesh into 2cm/¾in pieces. Add it to the stock, with the spring onions and chickpeas.

5 Return the shredded chicken to the pan, with salt and pepper to taste, and heat gently. When the soup is heated through, spoon into warmed bowls and serve.

ASPARAGUS with LEMON SAUCE

This is a good spring dish as the asparagus gives the immune system a kick start to help detoxify after winter. The sauce has a light, fresh taste and brings out the best in asparagus.

SERVES FOUR AS A FIRST COURSE

675g/1½lb asparagus, tough ends removed,
  and tied in a bundle
15ml/1 tbsp cornflour (cornstarch)
10ml/2 tsp unrefined sugar
2 egg yolks
juice of 1½ lemons
sea salt

COOK'S TIP
Use tiny asparagus spears as an elegant appetizer for a special dinner party.

1 Cook the bundle of asparagus in boiling salted water for 7–10 minutes.

2 Drain the asparagus well (reserving 200ml/7fl oz/scant 1 cup of the cooking liquid) and arrange the spears attractively in a serving dish. Set aside.

3 Blend the cornflour with the cooled, reserved cooking liquid and place in a small pan. Bring to the boil, stirring all the time with a wooden spoon, then cook over a gentle heat until the sauce thickens slightly. Stir in the sugar, then remove the pan from the heat and allow to cool slightly.

4 Beat the egg yolks thoroughly with the lemon juice and stir gradually into the cooled sauce. Cook the sauce over a very low heat, stirring all the time, until it thickens. Be careful not to overheat the sauce or it may curdle. Once the sauce has thickened, remove the pan from the heat and continue stirring for 1 minute. Season with salt or sugar if necessary. Allow the sauce to cool slightly.

5 Stir the cooled lemon sauce, then pour a little over the cooked asparagus. Cover and chill for at least 2 hours before serving accompanied by the rest of the lemon sauce.

BRAISED LEEKS with CARROTS

Sweet carrots and leeks go well together and are delicious finished with a little chopped mint or chervil. This is an easy accompaniment to roast lamb for a spring Sunday lunch.

SERVES SIX

65g/2½oz/5 tbsp butter or
   75ml/5 tbsp olive oil
675g/1½lb carrots, thickly sliced
2 fresh bay leaves
75ml/5 tbsp water
675g/1½lb leeks, cut into 5cm/
   2in lengths
120ml/4fl oz/½ cup white wine
30ml/2 tbsp chopped fresh mint
   or chervil
sea salt and ground black pepper

1 Heat 25g/1oz/2 tbsp of the butter or 30ml/2 tbsp of the oil in a pan and cook the carrots gently for 4–5 minutes.

2 Add the bay leaves, seasoning and the water to the pan. Bring to the boil, cover lightly and cook for 10–15 minutes until the carrots are tender. Uncover, then boil the cooking juices until they have all evaporated, leaving the carrots moist and glazed.

3 Meanwhile, heat another 25g/1oz/ 2 tbsp of the remaining butter or 30ml/2 tbsp of the oil in a deep frying pan or wide pan that will take the sliced leeks in a single layer. Add the leeks and fry them very gently in the melted butter over a medium to low heat for 4–5 minutes, without allowing them to turn brown.

4 Add seasoning, the wine and half the chopped herbs. Heat until simmering, then cover and cook gently for 5–8 minutes until the leeks are tender, but not collapsed.

5 Uncover the leeks and turn them in the buttery juices. Increase the heat slightly, then boil the liquid rapidly until reduced to a few tablespoons.

6 Add the carrots to the leeks and reheat them gently, then swirl in the remaining butter or oil.

7 Adjust the seasoning, if necessary. Transfer to a warmed serving dish and serve sprinkled with the remaining chopped herbs.

VARIATION
Braised leeks in tarragon cream
Cook 900g/2lb thoroughly washed, dried and sliced leeks in 40g/1½oz/3 tbsp butter or 45ml/3 tbsp olive oil as above. Season well with salt and pepper, add a pinch of sugar, 45ml/3 tbsp tarragon vinegar, 6 fresh tarragon sprigs and 60ml/4 tbsp white wine. Cover and cook as above over gentle heat. Add 150ml/¼ pint/⅔ cup double (heavy) cream or soya cream and allow to bubble and thicken. Season and sprinkle with chopped fresh tarragon.

GARGANELLI with SPRING VEGETABLES

Fresh, brightly coloured spring vegetables both look and taste good when served with pasta. A light sauce of dry white wine, extra virgin olive oil and fresh herbs is used to marry the two together for a delicious flavour.

SERVES FOUR

1 bunch asparagus, about 350g/12oz
4 young carrots
1 bunch spring onions (scallions)
130g/4½oz shelled fresh peas
350g/12oz/3 cups dried garganelli
60ml/4 tbsp dry white wine
90ml/6 tbsp extra virgin olive oil
a few sprigs fresh flat leaf parsley, mint and basil, leaves stripped and chopped
sea salt and ground black pepper
freshly grated Parmesan cheese or premium Italian-style vegetarian cheese, to serve

1 Trim off and discard the woody part of each asparagus stem, then cut off the tips on the diagonal. Cut the stems on the diagonal into 4cm/1½in pieces. Cut the carrots and spring onions on the diagonal into similar-size pieces.

2 Plunge the carrots, peas, asparagus stems and tips into a large pan of salted boiling water. Bring back to the boil, then reduce the heat and simmer for 8–10 minutes, until tender.

3 Meanwhile, cook the pasta in salted boiling water for 10–12 minutes, or according to the instructions on the packet, until just tender.

4 Drain the asparagus, carrots and peas and return them to the pan. Add the white wine, olive oil and salt and black pepper to taste, then gently toss over a medium to high heat until the wine has reduced and the vegetables glisten with the olive oil.

5 Drain the garganelli and transfer to a warmed large bowl. Add the vegetables, spring onions and sprigs of fresh herbs and toss well. Divide the pasta among four warmed individual plates and serve immediately, with freshly grated cheese.

COOK'S TIP
Garganelli are rolled short pasta shapes made with pasta dough enriched with egg. If you can't get garganelli, use another short shape, such as penne.

PENNE with CREAM and SMOKED SALMON

*This modern classic uses just three essential ingredients, which combine together
beautifully to make a quick and easy dish. Accompany with a green salad, ciabatta bread
and sparkling wine for a simple, quick and flavourful meal.*

SERVES FOUR

350g/12oz/3 cups dried penne or
   other pasta tubes
115g/4oz thinly sliced smoked salmon
2–3 fresh thyme sprigs
30ml/2 tbsp extra virgin olive oil
150ml/¼ pint/⅔ cup extra-thick
   single (light) cream or
   soya cream
sea salt and ground black pepper

1 Cook the dried pasta in a large pan of
lightly salted boiling water for 10 minutes
until it is just tender, or according to the
instructions on the packet.

2 Meanwhile, using sharp kitchen
scissors, cut the smoked salmon slices
into thin strips, about 5mm/¼in wide.
Strip the leaves from the thyme sprigs
and rinse them thoroughly in cold water.

3 Drain the pasta and return it to the
pan. Add the oil and heat gently, then
stir in the cream with about one-quarter
of the smoked salmon and thyme leaves,
then season with pepper. Heat gently
for 3–4 minutes, stirring all the time.
Check the seasoning. Divide the pasta
among four warmed bowls, top with
the remaining salmon and thyme leaves
and serve immediately.

VARIATION
Although white penne is the traditional pasta
to serve with this sauce, it also goes very
well with fresh wholemeal penne or ravioli
stuffed with spinach and ricotta cheese.

CHICKEN and ASPARAGUS RISOTTO

Use fairly thick asparagus in this classic springtime risotto, as fine spears tend to overcook. The thick ends of the asparagus are full of flavour and they become beautifully tender in the time it takes for the rice to absorb the stock.

SERVES FOUR

75ml/5 tbsp olive oil
1 leek, finely chopped
115g/4oz/1½ cups oyster or brown cap
   (cremini) mushrooms, sliced
3 skinless, boneless chicken breast
   fillets, cubed
350g/12oz asparagus
250g/9oz/1¼ cups risotto rice
900ml/1½ pints/3¾ cups simmering
   chicken stock
sea salt and ground black pepper
fresh Parmesan or premium
   Italian-style vegetarian cheese curls,
   to serve

1 Heat the olive oil in a pan. Add the finely chopped leek and cook gently until softened, but not coloured. Add the sliced mushrooms and cook for 5 minutes. Remove the vegetables from the pan and set aside.

2 Increase the heat and cook the cubes of chicken until golden on all sides. Do this in batches, if necessary, and then return them all to the pan.

3 Meanwhile, discard the woody ends from the asparagus and cut the spears in half. Set the tips aside. Cut the thick ends in half and add them to the pan. Return the leek and mushroom mixture to the pan and stir in the rice.

4 Pour in a ladleful of boiling stock and cook gently, stirring occasionally, until the stock is completely absorbed. Continue adding the stock a ladleful at a time, simmering until it is absorbed, the rice is tender and the chicken is cooked.

COOK'S TIP

To thoroughly remove all the soil from organic leeks, slice in half along their length and rinse under running water.

5 Add the asparagus tips with the last ladleful of boiling stock for the final 5 minutes and continue cooking the risotto very gently until the asparagus is tender. The whole process should take about 25–30 minutes.

6 Season the risotto to taste with salt and freshly ground black pepper and spoon it into individual warm serving bowls. Top each bowl with curls of cheese, and serve.

ESCALOPES of CHICKEN with VEGETABLES

This is a quick and light dish – ideal as the weather starts to warm up and easy meals become the order of the day. Flattening the chicken breasts thins and tenderizes the meat and also speeds up the cooking time.

SERVES FOUR

4 skinless, boneless chicken breast fillets,
 each weighing 175g/6oz
juice of 1 lime
120ml/4fl oz/½ cup olive oil
675g/1½lb mixed small new season
 potatoes, carrots, fennel (sliced
 if large), asparagus and peas
sea salt and ground black pepper
sprigs of fresh flat leaf parsley, to garnish

For the tomato mayonnaise
150ml/¼ pint/⅔ cup mayonnaise
15ml/1 tbsp sun-dried tomato
 purée (paste)

3 Meanwhile, put the potatoes and carrots in a pan with the remaining oil and season. Cover and cook for 10–15 minutes, stirring frequently.

4 Add the fennel and cook for a further 5 minutes, stirring frequently. Finally, add the asparagus and peas and cook for 5 minutes more, or until all the vegetables are tender and cooked.

5 To make the tomato mayonnaise, mix together the mayonnaise and sun-dried tomato purée in a small bowl. Spoon the vegetables on to a warmed serving platter or individual plates and arrange the chicken on top. Serve the tomato mayonnaise with the chicken and vegetables. Garnish with sprigs of flat leaf parsley.

1 Lay the chicken fillets between sheets of clear film (plastic wrap) or baking parchment and use a rolling pin to beat them until they are evenly thin. Season the chicken and sprinkle with the lime juice.

2 Heat 45ml/3 tbsp of the oil in a frying pan or griddle and cook the chicken escalopes for 10–12 minutes on each side, turning frequently.

COOK'S TIP
Any combinations of baby vegetables can be used. The weight specified is for prepared vegetables. Adjust the cooking time or the order in which they are added to the pan according to how long the chosen vegetables take to cook, for example add root vegetables first, before quick-cooking ones such as courgettes (zucchini), mangetouts (snow peas) or green beans.

ROAST LEG of LAMB

Tender young organic lamb is available only in the springtime, and is often served with a sauce using the first sprigs of mint of the year and early new potatoes. If you buy lamb at a farmers' market you can be happy in the knowledge that countryside seasons are being utilized and respected, and that the meat is fresh.

SERVES SIX

1.5kg/3¼lb leg of lamb
4 garlic cloves, sliced
2 fresh rosemary sprigs
30ml/2 tbsp light olive oil
300ml/½ pint/1¼ cups red wine
5ml/1 tsp honey
45ml/3 tbsp redcurrant jelly
sea salt and ground black pepper
spring vegetables, to serve

For the roast potatoes
45ml/3 tbsp olive oil
1.3kg/3lb potatoes, such as Desirée, peeled and cut into chunks

For the mint sauce
about 15g/½oz fresh mint
10ml/2 tsp unrefined caster (superfine) sugar
15ml/1 tbsp boiling water
30ml/2 tbsp white wine vinegar

1 Preheat the oven to 220°C/425°F/ Gas 7. Make small slits into the lamb all over the joint. Press a slice of garlic and a few rosemary leaves into each slit, then place the joint in a roasting pan and season well. Drizzle the oil over the lamb and roast for about 1 hour.

COOK'S TIP
To make a quick and tasty gravy from the pan juices, add about 300ml/½ pint/ 1¼ cups red wine, stock or water and boil, stirring occasionally, until reduced and well flavoured. Season to taste, then strain into a sauce boat to serve.

2 Meanwhile, mix the wine, honey and redcurrant jelly in a small pan and heat, stirring, until the jelly melts. Bring to the boil, then reduce the heat and simmer until reduced by half. Spoon this glaze over the lamb and return it to the oven for 30–45 minutes.

3 To make the potatoes, put the oil in a roasting pan on the shelf above the meat. Boil the potatoes for 5–10 minutes, then drain them and fluff up the surface of each with a fork.

4 Add the prepared potatoes to the hot oil and baste well, then roast them for 45 minutes, or until they are crisp.

5 While the potatoes are roasting, make the mint sauce. Place the mint on a chopping board and sprinkle the sugar over the top. Chop the mint finely, then transfer to a bowl.

6 Add the boiling water and stir until the sugar has dissolved. Add 15ml/1 tbsp vinegar and taste the sauce before adding the remaining vinegar. (You may want to add slightly less or more than the suggested quantity.) Leave the mint sauce to stand until you are ready to serve the meal.

7 Remove the lamb from the oven, cover it loosely with foil and set it aside in a warm place to rest for 10–15 minutes before carving. Serve with the crisp roast potatoes, mint sauce and a selection of seasonal spring vegetables.

COOK'S TIP
Lamb is the only farmed meat that still has a prime season. It is available all year around and is imported from all over the world. However, for best flavour it is better to wait for local stocks.

HERB-CRUSTED RACK of LAMB with PUY LENTILS

This lamb roast is quick and easy to prepare but looks impressive when served – it is the perfect choice when entertaining. Puy lentils have a strong earthy flavour that perfectly complements the rich lamb meat, and make a substantial and filling accompaniment.

SERVES FOUR

2 × 6-bone racks of lamb, chined
50g/2oz/1 cup fresh white or wholemeal
   (whole-wheat) breadcrumbs
2 large garlic cloves, crushed
90ml/6 tbsp chopped mixed fresh herbs,
   plus extra sprigs to garnish
50g/2oz/¼ cup butter, melted or
   50ml/3½ tbsp olive oil
sea salt and ground black pepper
new potatoes, to serve

For the Puy lentils
1 red onion, chopped
30ml/2 tbsp olive oil
400g/14oz can Puy lentils, rinsed
   and drained
400g/14oz can chopped tomatoes
30ml/2 tbsp chopped fresh flat leaf parsley

1 Preheat the oven to 220°C/425°F/ Gas 7. Trim any excess fat from the lamb, and season with salt and pepper.

2 Mix together the breadcrumbs, garlic, herbs and butter or oil, and press on to the fat-sides of the lamb. Place in a roasting pan and roast for 25 minutes. Cover with foil; stand for 5 minutes before carving.

3 Cook the onion in the olive oil until softened. Add the lentils and tomatoes and cook gently for 5 minutes, or until the lentils are piping hot. Stir in the parsley and season to taste.

4 Cut each rack of lamb in half and serve with the lentils and new potatoes. Garnish with herb sprigs.

LAMB BURGERS with RED ONION and TOMATO RELISH

Burgers made from lamb are a Middle Eastern creation. The spiciness of the burgers is complemented by the light, fresh herby relish. Serve with pitta bread and sour cream for an authentic taste, though baked potatoes and a crisp green salad are also good.

SERVES FOUR

25g/1oz/3 tbsp bulgur wheat
500g/1¼lb lean minced (ground) lamb
1 small red onion, finely chopped
2 garlic cloves, finely chopped
1 green chilli, seeded and finely chopped
5ml/1 tsp ground toasted cumin seeds
2.5ml/½ tsp ground sumac (optional)
15g/½oz/¼ cup chopped fresh flat
    leaf parsley
30ml/2 tbsp chopped fresh mint
olive oil, for frying
sea salt and ground black pepper

For the relish

2 red (bell) peppers, halved and seeded
2 red onions, cut into 5mm/¼in thick slices
75–90ml/5–6 tbsp extra virgin olive oil
350g/12oz cherry tomatoes, chopped
½–1 fresh red or green chilli, seeded
    and finely chopped (optional)
30ml/2 tbsp chopped fresh mint
30ml/2 tbsp chopped fresh parsley
15ml/1 tbsp chopped fresh oregano
    or marjoram
2.5–5ml/½–1 tsp each ground toasted
    cumin seeds
2.5–5ml/½–1 tsp sumac (optional)
juice of ½ lemon
unrefined caster (superfine) sugar,
    to taste

1 Pour 150ml/¼ pint/⅔ cup hot water over the bulgur wheat in a mixing bowl and leave to stand for 15 minutes, then drain the wheat in a sieve and squeeze out the excess moisture.

2 To make the relish, grill (broil) the peppers, skin side up, until the skin chars and blisters. Place in a bowl, cover and leave to stand for 10 minutes. Peel off the skin, dice the peppers finely and place in a bowl.

3 Brush the onions with 15ml/1 tbsp oil and grill for 5 minutes on each side, until browned. Leave to cool.

4 Place the bulgur in a bowl and add the minced lamb, onion, garlic, chilli, cumin, sumac, if using, parsley and mint. Mix the ingredients thoroughly together by hand, then season with 2.5ml/½ tsp salt and plenty of black pepper and mix again. Form the mixture into eight small burgers.

5 Chop the onions for the relish. Add with the tomatoes, chilli to taste, herbs and 2.5ml/½ tsp each of the cumin and sumac, if using, to the peppers. Stir in 60ml/4 tbsp of the remaining oil and 15ml/1 tbsp of the lemon juice. Season with salt, pepper and sugar and leave to stand for 20–30 minutes.

6 Heat a heavy frying pan over a high heat and grease lightly with olive oil. Cook the burgers for about 5–6 minutes on each side, or until just cooked at the centre.

7 While the burgers are cooking, taste the relish and adjust the seasoning, adding more pepper, sugar, oil, chilli, cumin, sumac, if using, and lemon juice to taste. Serve the burgers with the relish.

SALMON FISH CAKES

The secret of a good fish cake is to make it with freshly prepared fish and potatoes, home-made breadcrumbs and plenty of fresh herbs, such as dill and parsley or tarragon. Serve simply with rocket leaves and lemon wedges.

SERVES FOUR

450g/1lb cooked salmon fillet
450g/1lb freshly cooked potatoes, mashed
25g/1oz/2 tbsp butter, melted or
   30ml/2 tbsp olive oil
10ml/2 tsp wholegrain mustard
15ml/1 tbsp each chopped fresh dill and
   chopped fresh parsley or tarragon
grated rind and juice of ½ lemon
15g/½oz/2 tbsp wholemeal
   (whole-wheat) flour
1 egg, lightly beaten
150g/5oz/2 cups dried breadcrumbs
60ml/4 tbsp sunflower oil
sea salt and ground black pepper
rocket (arugula) leaves and chives, to garnish
lemon wedges, to serve

1 Flake the cooked salmon, discarding any skin and bones. Put it in a bowl with the mashed potato, melted butter or oil and wholegrain mustard, and mix well. Stir in the herbs and the lemon rind and juice. Season to taste with plenty of sea salt and ground black pepper.

2 Divide the mixture into eight portions and shape each into a ball, then flatten into a thick disc. Dip the fish cakes first in flour, then in egg and finally in breadcrumbs, making sure that they are evenly coated with crumbs.

3 Heat the oil in a frying pan until it is very hot. Fry the fish cakes in batches until golden brown and crisp all over. As each batch is ready, drain on kitchen paper and keep hot. Garnish with rocket and chives and serve with lemon wedges.

COOK'S TIP
Any fresh white or hot-smoked fish is suitable. Always buy organically farmed fish, or sustainably caught wild fish.

FILLETS of SEA BREAM in FILO PASTRY

Any firm fish fillets can be used for this dish – bass, grouper and red mullet or snapper are particularly good – and, as the number of organic seawater fish farms grows, an increasing variety of breeds is becoming available. Each parcel is a meal in itself and can be prepared several hours in advance.

3 Thinly slice the potatoes lengthways. Brush a baking sheet with a little of the oil. Lay a sheet of filo pastry on the sheet, brush it with oil, then lay a second sheet crossways over the first. Repeat with two more pastry sheets. Arrange a quarter of the sliced potatoes in the centre, season and add a quarter of the shredded sorrel. Lay a bream fillet on top, skin-side up. Season.

4 Loosely fold the filo pastry up and over to make a neat parcel. Make three more parcels; place on the baking sheet. Brush with half the melted butter or oil. Bake for about 20 minutes until the filo is puffed up and golden brown.

SERVES FOUR

8 small waxy salad potatoes,
    preferably red-skinned
200g/7oz sorrel, stalks removed
30ml/2 tbsp olive oil
16 filo pastry sheets, thawed if frozen
4 sea bream fillets, about 175g/6oz each,
    scaled but not skinned
50g/2oz/¼ cup butter, melted or
    60ml/4 tbsp olive oil
120ml/4fl oz/½ cup fish stock
250ml/8fl oz/1 cup whipping cream
    or soya cream
sea salt and ground black pepper
finely diced red (bell) pepper and
    salad leaves, to garnish

VARIATION

Use small spinach leaves or baby chard in place of the sorrel.

1 Preheat the oven to 200°C/400°F/ Gas 6. Cook the potatoes in a pan of lightly salted boiling water for about 20 minutes, or until just tender. Drain and leave to cool.

2 Set about half the sorrel leaves aside. Shred the remaining leaves by piling up six or eight at a time, rolling them up like a fat cigar and slicing them.

5 Meanwhile, make the sorrel sauce. Heat the remaining butter or oil in a pan, add the reserved sorrel and cook gently for 3 minutes, stirring, until it wilts. Stir in the stock and cream. Heat almost to boiling point, stirring so that the sorrel breaks down. Season to taste and keep hot until the fish parcels are ready. Serve garnished with red pepper and salad leaves. Hand round the sauce separately.

FROZEN CLEMENTINES

These pretty, sorbet-filled fruits store well in the freezer, so make them well in advance and they will be perfect for an impromptu dinner party. Organic citrus fruit has a matt skin – evidence that it has not been coated with shiny anti-fungal wax.

MAKES TWELVE

16 large clementines or small oranges
175g/6oz/scant 1 cup unrefined caster
    (superfine) sugar
105ml/7 tbsp water
juice of 2 lemons
a little fresh orange juice (if necessary)
fresh mint leaves, to decorate

1 Carefully slice the tops off 12 of the clementines to make lids. Place the lids on a baking sheet. Loosen the clementine flesh with a sharp knife then carefully scoop it out into a mixing bowl, keeping the shells intact. Scrape out as much of the membrane from the shells as possible. Place the shells on the baking tray and place the tray in the freezer.

2 Put the sugar and water in a heavy pan and heat gently, stirring until the sugar dissolves. Bring to the boil and boil for 3 minutes without stirring, then leave the syrup to cool. Stir in the lemon juice.

3 Grate the rind from the remaining four clementines. Squeeze the fruits and add the juice and rind to the lemon syrup.

4 Process the clementine flesh in a food processor or blender, then press it through a sieve (strainer) placed over a bowl to extract as much juice as possible. Add this to the syrup. You need about 900ml/1½ pints/3¾ cups of liquid. Make up to the required amount with fresh orange juice if necessary.

5 If making by hand, pour the mixture into a shallow plastic container and freeze for 3–4 hours, beating twice as the sorbet thickens to break up the ice crystals. If using an ice cream maker, churn the mixture until it holds its shape.

6 Gently pack the citrus sorbet into the clementine shells, mounding them up slightly in the centre. Position the lids on top and return the fruit to the freezer for several hours, or until the sorbet is frozen solid.

7 Transfer the frozen clementines to the refrigerator about 30 minutes before serving, to allow the sorbet to soften a little. Serve on individual plates and decorate with fresh mint leaves.

RHUBARB and GINGER ICE CREAM

The tangy combination of gently poached rhubarb and chopped ginger is blended with mascarpone to create this pretty blush-pink ice cream. Look for tender slim stalks of forced rhubarb in spring – it has a delicate pink colour and a delicious flavour.

SERVES FOUR TO SIX

5 pieces of preserved stem ginger
450g/1lb trimmed rhubarb, sliced
115g/4oz/generous ½ cup unrefined
    caster (superfine) sugar or rapadura
30ml/2 tbsp water
150g/5oz/⅔ cup mascarpone cheese
150ml/¼ pint/⅔ cup whipping cream
    or soya cream
wafer baskets, to serve (optional)

1 Using a sharp knife, roughly chop the preserved stem ginger and set it aside. Put the rhubarb slices into a pan and add the sugar and water. Bring to the boil, then cover and simmer for about 5 minutes until the rhubarb is just tender and still bright pink.

2 Tip the mixture into a food processor or blender, process until smooth, then leave to cool. Chill if time permits.

3 If making by hand, in a bowl, mix together the mascarpone, cream and stem ginger with the rhubarb purée. Pour the mixture into a plastic tub and freeze for 6 hours, or until firm, beating the mixture once or twice during the freezing time to break up the ice crystals.

COOK'S TIP
Rapadura is an alternative to refined sugar. It is made by sun-drying organic sugar cane juice and has a similar colour and texture to soft brown sugar, but has more flavour and is more nutritious.

4 If using an ice cream maker, churn the purée for 15–20 minutes until it is thick. Put the mascarpone into a bowl, soften it with a wooden spoon, then beat in the cream. Add the stem ginger, then churn in the ice cream maker until firm. Serve scoops of the ice cream in bowls or wafer baskets.

RICOTTA CHEESECAKE

This cheesecake makes good use of ricotta's firm texture. The irresistibly tangy filling is enriched with eggs and cream and enlivened with grated orange and lemon rind.

SERVES EIGHT

250g/11boz/2 cups ricotta cheese
120ml/4fl oz/½ cup double (heavy) cream
    or soya cream
2 eggs
1 egg yolk
75g/3oz/6 tbsp unrefined caster
    (superfine) sugar
finely grated rind of 1 orange and 1 lemon,
    plus extra to decorate

For the pastry
175g/6oz/1½ cups plain (all-purpose) flour
45ml/3 tbsp unrefined caster
    (superfine) sugar
115g/4oz/½ cup chilled butter, diced
1 egg yolk

1 To make the pastry, sift the flour and sugar on to a cold work surface. Make a well in the centre and add the butter and egg yolk. Work the flour into the butter and egg yolk.

2 Gather the dough together, reserve a quarter of it and press the rest of the dough into a 23cm/9in fluted flan tin (quiche pan) with a removable base, and chill.

3 Preheat the oven to 190°C/375°F/ Gas 5. Put the cheese, cream, eggs and egg yolk, sugar and citrus rinds in a large bowl and beat well.

4 Prick the bottom of the pastry case, then line with foil and fill with baking beans. Bake for 15 minutes, transfer to a wire rack, remove the foil and beans and allow the pastry to cool in the tin.

5 Spoon the cheese and cream filling into the pastry case and level the surface. Roll out the reserved dough and cut into long, even strips. Arrange the strips on the top of the filling in a lattice pattern, sticking them in place with water.

6 Bake the cheesecake for 30–35 minutes until golden and set. Transfer to a wire rack and leave to cool, then carefully remove the side of the tin. Use a palette knife (metal spatula) to transfer the tart to a serving plate. Decorate with citrus rind before serving.

VARIATIONS
• Add 50g/2oz/⅓ cup plain (semisweet) chocolate chips to the filling in step 3.
• Sprinkle 75g/3oz sultanas (golden raisins) into the pastry case before filling.

CITRUS SPONGE

This cake is a light and airy whisked sponge made with matzo and potato flours rather than traditional wheat flour. Serve it as a dessert or as a cake, with coffee.

SERVES SIX TO EIGHT

12 eggs, separated
300g/11oz/1½ cups unrefined caster
   (superfine) sugar
120ml/4fl oz/½ cup fresh orange juice
grated rind of 1 orange
grated rind of 1 lemon
50g/2oz/½ cup potato flour, sifted
90g/3½oz/¾ cup fine matzo meal or
   matzo meal flour, sifted
unrefined icing (confectioners') sugar,
   for dusting
orange juice and segments of orange,
   to serve

1 Preheat the oven to 160°C/325°F/ Gas 3. Whisk the egg yolks until pale and frothy, then whisk in the sugar, orange juice, orange rind and lemon rind.

2 Fold the sifted flours or flour and meal into the egg and sugar mixture. In a clean bowl, whisk the egg whites until stiff, then fold into the egg yolk mixture.

VARIATION
Omit the lemon and replace the orange with two blood oranges for a really fresh, fruity flavour.

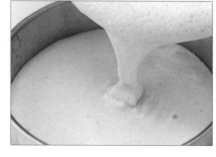

3 Pour the cake mixture into a deep, ungreased 25cm/10in cake tin (pan) and bake for about 1 hour, or until a cocktail stick (toothpick), inserted in the centre, comes out clean. Leave to cool in the tin.

4 When cold, turn out the cake and invert on to a serving plate. Dust with a little icing sugar and serve in wedges with orange segments, moistened with a little fresh orange juice.

COOK'S TIPS
• When testing to see if the cake is cooked, if you don't have a cocktail stick to hand, use a strand of raw dried spaghetti instead – it will work just as well.
• If you cannot find organic matzo meal, try fine polenta instead.

SUMMER

The abundance of fresh produce at this time of year makes summer a wonderful time for any cook. With hot, sunny days and long, balmy evenings for picnics and barbecues, summer eating is a sheer delight. Chilled dishes are easy to prepare in advance. Take your pick from the wide selection of classic colourful salads — including Middle Eastern Tabbouleh, Country Pasta Salad — to make the most of the dazzling array of organic fruit and vegetables available now. For a superb main course that will feed plenty, try Olive Oil Roasted Chicken with Summer Vegetables and accompany it with organic bread and a crisp and refreshing white wine. With a wide selection of mouthwatering and juicy fruits in season, summer desserts really are special. Try refreshing Frozen Melon or, if you want something really indulgent, Coffee Crêpes with Peaches and Cream, or Blueberry Frangipane Flan. Summer is also the beginning of the preserving season and you just can't beat home-made strawberry jam served with freshly baked scones and cream – delicious!

TABBOULEH

This is a wonderfully refreshing, tangy salad of soaked bulgur wheat with masses of fresh organic mint and parsley. Increase the amount of fresh herbs for a greener salad.

SERVES FOUR TO SIX

250g/9oz/1½ cups bulgur wheat
1 large bunch spring onions (scallions),
    thinly sliced
1 cucumber, finely chopped or diced
3 tomatoes, chopped
1.5–2.5ml/¼–½ tsp ground cumin
1 large bunch fresh flat leaf
    parsley, chopped
1 large bunch fresh mint, chopped
juice of 2 lemons, or to taste
60ml/4 tbsp extra virgin olive oil
cos or romaine lettuce leaves
olives, lemon wedges, tomato wedges,
    cucumber slices and mint sprigs,
    to garnish (optional)
natural (plain) yogurt, to serve (optional)

1 Pick over the bulgur wheat to remove any dirt. Place it in a bowl, cover with cold water and leave to soak for about 30 minutes. Transfer the bulgur wheat to a sieve (strainer) and drain well, shaking to remove any excess water, then return it to the bowl.

2 Add the spring onions to the bulgur wheat, then mix and squeeze together with your hands to combine.

3 Add the cucumber, tomatoes, cumin, parsley, mint, lemon juice and oil to the bulgur wheat and toss well.

4 Heap the tabbouleh on to a bed of lettuce leaves and garnish with olives, lemon wedges, tomato, cucumber and mint sprigs, if you like. Serve with a bowl of natural yogurt, if you like.

VARIATION
Use couscous soaked in boiling water in place of the bulgur wheat and use fresh coriander (cilantro) instead of parsley.

TOMATO and MOZZARELLA SALAD

Sweet, naturally ripened organic tomatoes and fresh basil capture the essence of summer in this simple salad. Choose plum or beefsteak tomatoes for this dish.

SERVES FOUR

5 ripe tomatoes
2 × 225g/8oz buffalo mozzarella cheeses,
   drained and sliced
1 small red onion, chopped

For the dressing
½ small garlic clove, peeled
15g/½oz/½ cup fresh basil leaves
30ml/2 tbsp chopped fresh flat
   leaf parsley
25ml/1½ tbsp small salted capers, rinsed
2.5ml/½ tsp mustard
75–90ml/5–6 tbsp extra virgin olive oil
5–10ml/1–2 tsp balsamic vinegar
ground black pepper

For the garnish
fresh basil leaves
fresh parsley sprigs

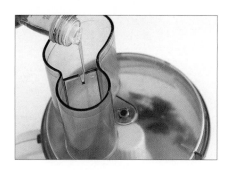

1 First make the dressing. Put the garlic, basil, parsley, half the capers and the mustard in a food processor or blender and process briefly to chop. Then, with the motor running, gradually pour in the olive oil through the feeder tube to make a smooth purée with a dressing consistency. Add the balsamic vinegar to taste and season with plenty of ground black pepper.

2 Slice the tomatoes. Arrange the tomato and mozzarella slices on a plate. Scatter the onion over and season with a little ground black pepper.

3 Drizzle the dressing over the salad, then scatter a few basil leaves, parsley sprigs and the remaining capers on top as a garnish. Leave for 10–15 minutes before serving.

SUMMER SALAD

Ripe organic tomatoes, mozzarella and olives make a good base for a fresh and flavourful pasta salad that is perfect for a light summer lunch.

SERVES FOUR

350g/12oz/3 cups dried penne
150g/5oz packet buffalo mozzarella,
    drained and diced
3 ripe tomatoes, diced
10 pitted black olives, sliced
10 pitted green olives, sliced
1 spring onion (scallion), thinly sliced on
    the diagonal
a handful fresh basil leaves

For the dressing
90ml/6 tbsp extra virgin olive oil
15ml/1 tbsp balsamic vinegar or
    lemon juice
sea salt and ground black pepper

COOK'S TIP
Mozzarella made from buffalo milk
has more flavour than the type made
with cow's milk. It is widely available in
large supermarkets.

1 Cook the pasta for 10–12 minutes, or according to the instructions on the packet. Pour it into a colander and rinse briefly under cold running water, then [sha]ke the colander to remove as much [wate]r as possible and leave to drain.

[VAR]IATION
[Mak]e the salad more substantial by adding [s]liced peppers, flaked tuna, anchovy fillets or diced ham. Always choose sustainably caught tuna and anchovies.

2 Make the dressing. Whisk the olive oil and balsamic vinegar or lemon juice in a jug (pitcher) with a little salt and pepper to taste.

3 Place the pasta, mozzarella, tomatoes, olives and spring onion in a large bowl, pour the dressing over and toss together well. Taste for seasoning before serving, sprinkled with basil leaves.

COUNTRY PASTA SALAD

Colourful, tasty and nutritious, this is the ideal pasta salad for a summer picnic. A variety of organic pasta types are available – any medium-size shapes are suitable for this salad.

SERVES SIX

300g/11oz/2¾ cups dried fusilli
150g/5oz fine green beans,
    trimmed and cut into
    5cm/2in lengths
1 potato, about 150g/5oz, diced
200g/7oz cherry tomatoes, halved
2 spring onions (scallions),
    finely chopped
90g/3½oz/scant 1¼ cups Parmesan
    cheese or premium Italian-style
    vegetarian cheese, coarsely shaved
6–8 pitted black olives, cut into rings
15–30ml/1–2 tbsp capers, to taste

For the dressing
90ml/6 tbsp extra virgin olive oil
15ml/1 tbsp balsamic vinegar
15ml/1 tbsp chopped fresh flat leaf parsley
sea salt and ground black pepper

1 Cook the pasta according to the instructions on the packet. Drain it into a colander, rinse under cold running water until cold, then shake the colander to remove as much water as possible. Leave to drain and dry.

2 Cook the beans and diced potato in a pan of boiling water for 5–6 minutes or steam for 8–10 minutes. Drain and let cool.

3 To make the dressing, put all the ingredients in a large bowl with a little sea salt and ground black pepper to taste and whisk well to mix.

4 Add the tomatoes, spring onions, Parmesan, olive rings and capers to the dressing then stir in the cold pasta, beans and potato. Toss well to mix. Cover and leave to stand for about 30 minutes. Taste for seasoning before serving.

VARIATIONS
Use pasta shapes, such as conchiglie or penne, instead of fusilli. Try wholemeal pasta shapes for a nuttier taste. Other summer vegetables – steamed courgettes (zucchini) or mangetouts (snow peas), or roasted red (bell) peppers – all taste wonderful in this salad.

GRILLED VEGETABLE PIZZA

You really can't go too far wrong with this classic mixture of Mediterranean grilled vegetables on home-made pizza dough. It is filling and healthy, and is a favourite with children.

3 Place the pizza dough on a sheet of baking parchment on a baking sheet and roll or gently press it out to form a 25cm/10in round, making the edges slightly thicker than the centre.

4 Lightly brush the pizza dough with any remaining oil, then spread the chopped plum tomatoes evenly over the dough.

SERVES SIX

1 courgette (zucchini), sliced
2 baby aubergines (eggplant) or
   1 small aubergine, sliced
30ml/2 tbsp olive oil
1 yellow (bell) pepper, seeded and sliced
115g/4oz/1 cup cornmeal
50g/2oz/½ cup potato flour
50g/2oz/½ cup soya flour
5ml/1 tsp baking powder
2.5ml/½ tsp sea salt
50g/2oz/¼ cup non-hydrogenated margarine
about 105ml/7 tbsp milk
4 plum tomatoes, skinned and chopped
30ml/2 tbsp chopped fresh basil
115g/4oz buffalo mozzarella cheese, sliced
sea salt and ground black pepper
fresh basil sprigs, to garnish

1 Preheat the grill (broiler). Brush the courgette and aubergine slices with a little oil and place on a grill rack with the pepper slices. Cook under the grill until lightly browned, turning once.

2 Meanwhile, preheat the oven to 200°C/400°F/Gas 6. Place the cornmeal, potato flour, soya flour, baking powder and salt in a mixing bowl and stir to mix. Lightly rub in the margarine until the mixture resembles coarse breadcrumbs, then stir in enough of the milk to make a soft but not sticky dough.

VARIATION
Top the pizza with 115g/4oz sliced goat's cheese instead of the mozzarella for a creamy alternative.

5 Sprinkle with the chopped basil and season with salt and pepper. Arrange the grilled vegetables over the tomatoes and top with the cheese.

6 Bake for 25–30 minutes until crisp and golden brown. Garnish the pizza with fresh basil sprigs and serve immediately, cut into slices.

COOK'S TIP
This recipe uses a combination of different types of flour to give an interesting flavour and texture to the base. If you prefer, use 225g/8oz/2 cups of plain (all-purpose) flour or a combination of half plain and half wholemeal (whole-wheat) flours.

SPICED VEGETABLE COUSCOUS

*This tasty vegetarian main course is easy to make and can be prepared with any
number of seasonal organic vegetables such as spinach, peas, broad beans or corn.*

SERVES SIX

45ml/3 tbsp olive oil
1 large onion, finely chopped
2 garlic cloves, crushed
15ml/1 tbsp tomato purée (paste)
2.5ml/½ tsp ground turmeric
2.5ml/½ tsp cayenne pepper
5ml/1 tsp ground coriander
5ml/1 tsp ground cumin
225g/8oz/1½ cups cauliflower florets
225g/8oz baby carrots, trimmed
1 red (bell) pepper, seeded and diced
225g/8oz courgettes (zucchini), sliced
400g/14oz can chickpeas, drained
   and rinsed
4 beefsteak tomatoes, skinned and sliced
45ml/3 tbsp chopped fresh coriander
   (cilantro)
sea salt and ground black pepper
coriander sprigs, to garnish

For the couscous
2.5ml/½ tsp sea salt
450g/1lb/2⅔ cups couscous
50g/2oz/¼ cup butter or
   50ml/3½ tbsp sunflower oil

1 Heat 30ml/2 tbsp oil in a large pan, add the onion and garlic and cook until soft and translucent. Stir in the tomato purée, turmeric, cayenne, coriander and cumin. Cook, stirring, for 2 minutes.

2 Add the cauliflower, baby carrots and pepper, with enough water to come halfway up the vegetables. Bring to the boil, then lower the heat, cover and simmer for 10 minutes.

3 Add the courgettes, chickpeas and tomatoes to the pan and cook for 10 minutes. Stir in the fresh coriander and season. Keep hot.

4 To cook the couscous, bring about 475ml/16fl oz/2 cups water to the boil in a large pan. Add the remaining olive oil and the salt. Remove from the heat and add the couscous, stirring. Allow to swell for 2 minutes.

5 Add the butter or sunflower oil, and heat through gently, stirring to separate the grains.

6 Turn the couscous out on to a warm serving dish, and spoon the cooked vegetables on top, pouring over any liquid. Garnish with coriander and serve immediately.

OLIVE OIL ROASTED CHICKEN with SUMMER VEGETABLES

This is a delicious alternative to a traditional roast chicken. Organic chicken can be so much tastier and more tender than intensively reared poultry, especially if the birds are raised biodynamically.

SERVES FOUR

1.8–2kg/4–4½lb roasting chicken
150ml/¼ pint/⅔ cup extra virgin olive oil
½ lemon
few sprigs of fresh thyme
450g/1lb small new potatoes
1 aubergine (eggplant), cut into
   2.5cm/1in dice
1 red (bell) pepper, seeded and quartered
1 fennel bulb, trimmed and quartered
8 large garlic cloves, unpeeled
coarse sea salt and ground black pepper

1 Preheat the oven to 200°C/400°F/ Gas 6. Rub the chicken all over with olive oil and season with pepper. Place the lemon half inside the bird, with a sprig or two of thyme. Put the chicken breast side down in a large roasting pan. Roast for about 30 minutes.

2 Remove the chicken from the oven and season with salt. Turn the chicken right side up, and baste. Surround the bird with the potatoes, roll them in the pan juices, and return to the oven.

3 After 30 minutes, add the aubergine, red pepper, fennel and garlic cloves to the pan. Drizzle with the remaining oil, and season with salt and pepper. Add any remaining thyme to the vegetables. Return to the oven, and cook for about 40 minutes more, basting and turning the vegetables occasionally.

4 To find out if the chicken is cooked, push the tip of a sharp knife between the thigh and breast. If the juices run clear, it is done. The vegetables should be tender and just beginning to brown. Serve the chicken and vegetables from the pan, or transfer the vegetables to a serving dish, joint the chicken and place it on top. Serve the skimmed juices in a gravy boat.

VARIATION

Serve rosemary potato wedges with the chicken. Heat 60ml/4 tbsp olive oil for 10 minutes in a roasting pan in an oven preheated to 200°C/400°F/Gas 6. Cut the potatoes into wedges and add to the oil. Sprinkle over 10ml/2 tsp dried rosemary. Season and bake for 50–60 minutes.

FRUIT COMPOTE with CHOCOLATE MERINGUES

Mini chocolate meringues are sandwiched with crème fraîche and served with a compote of mixed summer berries to make this impressive dessert.

3 Carefully spoon the meringue into a large piping (pastry) bag fitted with a large star nozzle. Pipe small round whirls of the mixture on to the prepared baking sheets.

4 Bake the meringues for 2½–3 hours until they are firm and crisp. Remove from the oven. Carefully peel the meringues off the paper, then transfer them to a wire rack to cool.

5 To make the compote, heat the fruit juices in a small pan with the honey until almost boiling.

6 Place the mixed berries in a bowl and pour over the hot fruit juice and honey mixture. Stir gently to mix, then set aside and leave to cool. Once cool, cover the bowl with clear film (plastic wrap) and chill until required.

7 When ready to serve, gently sandwich the meringues together with the crème fraîche and arrange on a serving plate.

8 Serve the meringues immediately, topping each serving of the mixed fruit compote with the meringues.

SERVES SIX

105ml/7 tbsp unsweetened red grape juice
105ml/7 tbsp unsweetened apple juice
30ml/2 tbsp clear honey
450g/1lb/4 cups mixed fresh summer
  berries, such as blackcurrants,
  redcurrants, raspberries
  and blackberries

For the meringues
3 egg whites
175g/6oz/¾ cup unrefined caster
  (superfine) sugar
75g/3oz good-quality plain (semisweet)
  chocolate, finely grated
175g/6oz/scant 1 cup crème fraîche

1 Preheat the oven to 110°C/225°F/ Gas ¼. Grease and line two large baking sheets with baking parchment.

2 To make the meringues, whisk the egg whites in a mixing bowl until stiff. Gradually whisk in half the sugar, then fold in the remaining sugar, using a metal spoon. Fold in the grated chocolate.

FROZEN MELON

Freezing sorbet in hollowed out fruit, which is then cut into icy wedges, is an excellent idea. The refreshing flavour makes this dessert irresistible on a hot summer's day.

SERVES SIX

50g/2oz/¼ cup unrefined caster
   (superfine) sugar
30ml/2 tbsp clear honey
15ml/1 tbsp lemon juice
60ml/4 tbsp water
1 medium cantaloupe melon or Charentais
   melon, about 1 kg/2¼lb
crushed ice, cucumber slices and borage
   flowers, to decorate

1 Put the sugar, honey, lemon juice and water in a heavy pan, and heat gently until the sugar dissolves. Bring to the boil, and boil for 1 minute, without stirring, to make a syrup. Leave to cool.

2 Cut the melon in half and discard the seeds. Carefully scoop out the flesh using a metal spoon or melon baller and place in a food processor, taking care to keep the halved shells intact.

3 Blend the melon flesh until very smooth, then transfer to a mixing bowl. Stir in the cooled sugar syrup and chill until very cold. Invert the melon shells and leave them to drain on kitchen paper for a few minutes, then transfer them to the freezer while making the sorbet.

4 If making by hand, pour the mixture into a container and freeze for 3–4 hours, beating well twice with a fork, a whisk or in a food processor, to break up the ice crystals and produce a smooth texture. If using an ice cream maker, churn the melon mixture in the ice cream maker until the sorbet holds its shape.

5 Pack the sorbet into the melon shells and level the surface with a knife. Use a dessertspoon to scoop out the centre of each filled melon shell to simulate the seed cavity. Freeze the prepared fruit overnight until firm.

6 To serve, use a large knife to cut each melon half into three wedges. Serve on a bed of ice on a large platter or individual serving plates, and decorate with the cucumber slices and borage flowers.

COOK'S TIP
If the melon sorbet is too firm to cut when taken straight from the freezer, let it soften in the refrigerator for 10–20 minutes. Take care when slicing the frozen melon shell into wedges. A serrated kitchen knife is easier to work with.

SUMMER BERRIES in WARM SABAYON GLAZE

This luxurious combination of summer berries under a light and fluffy alcoholic sauce is lightly grilled to form a crisp, caramelized topping.

SERVES FOUR

450g/1lb/4 cups mixed summer berries, or other soft fruit
4 egg yolks
50g/2oz/¼ cup unrefined caster (superfine) sugar
120ml/4fl oz/½ cup white dessert wine, plus extra to serve (optional)
a little unrefined icing (confectioners') sugar, sifted, and mint leaves, to decorate (optional)

COOK'S TIP
If you want to omit the alcohol, use a pure fruit juice instead, such as grape, mango or apricot.

1 Arrange the fruit in four flameproof dishes. Preheat the grill (broiler).

2 Whisk the egg yolks in a large bowl with the sugar and wine. Place the bowl over a pan of hot water and whisk constantly until thick, fluffy and pale.

3 Pour equal quantities of the sabayon sauce into each dish. Place under the grill for 1–2 minutes until just turning brown. Sprinkle the fruit with icing sugar and sprinkle with mint leaves just before serving, if you like. Add an extra splash of wine to the dishes, if you like.

COFFEE CRÊPES with PEACHES and CREAM

Juicy golden organic peaches and cream conjure up the sweet taste of summer. Here they are delicious as the filling for these light coffee-flavoured buckwheat crêpes.

SERVES SIX

75g/3oz/⅔ cup plain (all-purpose) flour
25g/1oz/¼ cup buckwheat flour
1 egg, beaten
200ml/7fl oz/scant 1 cup milk or
    soya milk
15g/½oz/1 tbsp butter, melted
100ml/3½fl oz/scant ½ cup brewed
    coffee, cooled
sunflower oil, for frying

For the filling
6 ripe peaches
300ml/½ pint/1¼ cups double
    (heavy) cream
15ml/1 tbsp brandy
225g/8oz/1 cup crème fraîche
65g/2½oz/generous ¼ cup unrefined
    caster (superfine) sugar
30ml/2 tbsp unrefined icing
    (confectioners') sugar, for dusting
    (optional)

1 Sift the flours into a mixing bowl. Make a well in the middle and add the beaten egg, half the milk and the melted butter. Gradually mix in the flour, beating until the mixture is smooth, then beat in the remaining milk and the coffee.

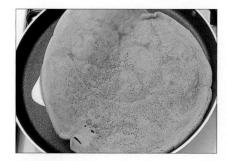

2 Heat a drizzle of sunflower oil in a 15–20cm/6–8in crêpe pan. Pour in just enough batter to cover the base of the pan thinly, swirling the pan to spread the mixture evenly. Cook for 2–3 minutes until the underneath is golden brown, then flip the crêpe over using a metal spatula and cook the other side.

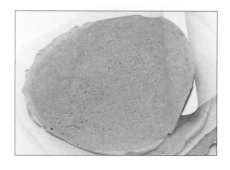

3 Slide the crêpe out of the pan on to a plate. Continue making crêpes until all the mixture is used, stacking and interleaving them with baking parchment to keep them separate.

4 To make the filling, halve the peaches and carefully remove the stones. Cut the peaches into thick slices. Whip the cream and brandy together until soft peaks form. Beat the crème fraîche with the sugar until smooth. Beat 30ml/2 tbsp of the cream into the crème fraîche, then fold in the remainder.

5 Place six of the crêpes on individual serving plates. Spoon a little of the brandy cream on to one half of each crêpe and top with peach slices. Gently fold the crêpe over and dust with a little sifted icing sugar, if you like. Serve immediately.

BLUEBERRY FRANGIPANE FLAN

A tangy lemon pastry case is filled with a nutty sweet almond filling dotted with ripe blueberries. Their wonderful colour and taste make blueberries a seasonal favourite.

SERVES SIX

30ml/2 tbsp ground coffee
45ml/3 tbsp milk or soya milk
50g/2oz/¼ cup unsalted (sweet) butter
50g/2oz/¼ cup unrefined caster
   (superfine) sugar
I egg
115g/4oz/I cup ground almonds
15ml/I tbsp plain (all-purpose)
   flour, sifted
225g/8oz/2 cups blueberries
30ml/2 tbsp jam
15ml/I tbsp brandy
crème fraîche or sour cream, to serve

For the pastry
175g/6oz/1½ cups plain (all-purpose) flour
115g/4oz/½ cup unsalted (sweet) butter or
   non-hydrogenated margarine
25g/1oz/2 tbsp unrefined caster
     (superfine) sugar
finely grated rind of ½ lemon
15ml/I tbsp chilled water

I Preheat the oven to 190°C/375°F/ Gas 5. To make the pastry, sift the flour into a bowl and rub in the butter. Stir in the sugar and lemon rind, then add the water and mix to a firm dough. Wrap the dough in clear film (plastic wrap) and chill for 20 minutes.

2 Roll out the pastry on a lightly floured work surface and use to line a 23cm/9in loose-based flan tin (quiche pan). Line the pastry with baking parchment and baking beans and bake for 10 minutes. Remove the paper and beans and bake for a further 10 minutes. Remove from the oven.

3 Meanwhile, to make the filling, put the ground coffee in a bowl. Bring the milk almost to the boil, then pour over the coffee and leave to infuse for 4 minutes. Cream the butter and sugar until pale. Beat in the egg, then add the almonds and flour. Strain the coffee-flavoured milk through a sieve (strainer) and fold in.

4 Spoon the coffee mixture into the pastry case and spread evenly. Sprinkle the blueberries over the top and push them down slightly into the mixture. Bake for 30 minutes, until firm, covering with foil after 20 minutes.

5 Remove the tart from the oven and allow to cool slightly. Heat the jam and brandy in a small pan until melted. Brush over the flan and remove from the tin. Serve warm with crème fraîche or sour cream.

SCONES with STRAWBERRY JAM

There is not much that can beat freshly made scones with good quality jam. Making your own is not difficult and their flavour really will be much better than bought varieties.

MAKES ABOUT 1.3KG/3LB JAM
AND 10–12 SCONES

For the strawberry jam
1kg/2¼lb/9 cups small strawberries
900g/2lb/4½ cups granulated (white) sugar
juice of 2 lemons

For the scones
225g/8oz/2 cups plain (all-purpose) flour
15ml/1 tbsp baking powder
50g/2oz/¼ cup butter or
    non-hydrogenated margarine, diced
1 egg, beaten, plus extra to glaze
75ml/5 tbsp milk or soya milk
clotted or double (heavy) cream, to serve

1 Layer the strawberries and sugar in a large bowl. Cover and leave overnight.

2 The next day, transfer the strawberries and their juice to a large heavy pan. Add the lemon juice. Bring to the boil, stirring until the sugar has dissolved.

3 Boil steadily for 10–15 minutes. Spoon a small amount on to a chilled saucer. Chill for 3 minutes, then push the jam with your finger; if wrinkles form, it is ready. Cool for 10 minutes.

4 Pour the strawberry jam into warm, sterilized jars, filling them right to the top. Cover the jam with a disc of waxed paper, waxed side down, and seal the jar with a damp cellophane round and secure with an elastic band while the jam is still hot. Label when the jars are cold. The jam can be stored in a cool dark place, and it should keep for up to 1 year.

5 To make the scones, preheat the oven to 220°C/425°F/Gas 7. Butter a baking sheet. Sift the flour and baking powder together, then rub in the butter or margarine. Make a well in the centre of the flour mixture, add the egg and milk and mix to a soft dough using a fork or a round-bladed knife.

6 Turn out the scone dough on to a floured surface, and knead very lightly until smooth. Roll out the dough to about a 2cm/¾in thickness and cut into 10 or 12 rounds using a 5cm/2in plain or fluted cutter dipped in flour.

7 Transfer to the baking sheet, brush the tops with egg, then bake for about 8 minutes, until risen and golden. Cool slightly on a wire rack then serve with the jam and clotted or double cream.

AUTUMN

As the nights start to draw in, warming dishes become popular, so why not make the most of hearty organic vegetables such as parsnips, squashes and potatoes? Try Roasted Garlic and Squash Soup with roasted tomato salsa, or Potatoes and Parsnips Baked with Garlic and Cream. Delicious fish dishes to try now include Sole with Wild Mushrooms or Potato-topped Fish Pie served simply with roasted root vegetables. Autumn orchards and hedgerows provide a wonderful array of fresh fruits such as organic apples, plums and pears that are full of flavour and popular in both sweet and savoury dishes. Try Duck Sausages with Spicy Plum Sauce, or Spicy Venison Casserole with cranberries and orange. Sticky Pear Pudding is a delicious sweet treat, while individual Hot Blackberry and Apple Soufflés are just right for a dinner party. Freshly baked cakes are especially satisfying at this time of year; try Parsnip Cake with Orange Icing. And for an instant treat that is satisfying and filling make Oat and Raisin Drop Scones served warm straight from the griddle for a real taste of autumn.

CLAM, MUSHROOM and POTATO CHOWDER

Members of the same family as mussels, scallops and oysters, clams have a sweet flavour and firm texture, which combine beautifully with wild mushrooms in this filling soup.

SERVES 4

48 clams, scrubbed
50g/2oz/¼ cup unsalted (sweet) butter
    or non-hydrogenated margarine
1 large onion, chopped
1 celery stick, sliced
1 carrot, sliced
225g/8oz/3¾ cups assorted wild and
    cultivated mushrooms
225g/8oz floury potatoes (such as
    Maris Piper or King Edward),
    thickly sliced
1.2 litres/2 pints/5 cups boiling light
    chicken or vegetable stock
1 thyme sprig
4 parsley stalks
sea salt and ground black pepper
thyme sprigs, to garnish

1 Place the clams in a large, heavy pan, discarding any that are open. Add 1cm/½in of water to the pan, then cover and bring to the boil. Cook the clams over a medium heat for 6–8 minutes, shaking the pan occasionally, until the clams open (discard any clams that do not open).

2 Drain the clams over a bowl and remove most of the shells, leaving some in the shells as a garnish. Strain the cooking juices into the bowl, add all the clams and set aside.

3 Add the butter, onion, celery and carrot to the pan and cook gently until just softened but not coloured. Add the wild and cultivated mushrooms and cook for 3–4 minutes until their juices begin to appear. Add the potato slices, the clams and their juices, the stock, thyme and parsley stalks.

4 Bring to the boil, then reduce the heat, cover and simmer for 25 minutes. Season to taste, ladle into soup bowls, and garnish with thyme sprigs.

ROASTED GARLIC and SQUASH SOUP

This is a wonderful, richly flavoured dish. A spoonful of hot and spicy tomato salsa gives bite to this sweet-tasting butternut squash and garlic soup.

SERVES FOUR TO FIVE

2 garlic bulbs, outer papery
   skin removed
75ml/5 tbsp olive oil
a few fresh thyme sprigs
1 large butternut squash, halved
   and seeded
2 onions, chopped
5ml/1 tsp ground coriander
1.2 litres/2 pints/5 cups vegetable or
   chicken stock
30–45ml/2–3 tbsp chopped fresh oregano
   or marjoram
sea salt and ground black pepper

For the salsa
4 large ripe tomatoes, halved and seeded
1 red (bell) pepper, halved and seeded
1 large fresh red chilli, halved and seeded
30–45ml/2–3 tbsp extra virgin olive oil
15ml/1 tbsp balsamic vinegar

1 Preheat the oven to 220°C/425°F/ Gas 7. Place the garlic bulbs on a piece of foil and pour over half the olive oil. Add the thyme sprigs, then fold the foil around the garlic bulbs to enclose them completely. Place the foil parcel on a baking sheet with the butternut squash and brush the squash with 15ml/1 tbsp of the remaining olive oil. Add the halved and seeded tomatoes, red pepper and fresh chilli for the salsa.

2 Roast the vegetables for 25 minutes, then remove the tomatoes, pepper and chilli. Reduce the temperature to 190°C/ 375°F/Gas 5 and cook the squash and garlic for 20–25 minutes more, or until the squash is tender.

3 Heat the remaining oil in a large, heavy pan and cook the onions and ground coriander gently for about 10 minutes, or until softened.

4 Skin the pepper and chilli and process in a food processor or blender with the tomatoes and 30ml/2 tbsp olive oil. Stir in the vinegar and seasoning to taste. Add the remaining oil if you think the salsa needs it.

5 Squeeze the roasted garlic out of its papery skin into the onions. Scoop the squash out of its skin and add it to the pan. Add the vegetable or chicken stock, 2.5ml/½ tsp salt and plenty of black pepper. Bring to the boil and simmer for 10 minutes.

6 Stir in half the chopped fresh oregano or marjoram and allow the soup to cool slightly, then process it in batches if necessary, in a food processor or blender until smooth. Alternatively, press the soup through a fine sieve (strainer).

7 Reheat the soup in a clean pan without allowing it to boil, then taste for seasoning before ladling it into individual warmed bowls. Top each with a spoonful of the tomato salsa and sprinkle over the remaining chopped fresh oregano or marjoram. Serve immediately.

GARLIC CHIVE RICE with MUSHROOMS

A wide range of organic mushrooms is readily available. They combine well with rice and garlic chives to make a tasty accompaniment to vegetarian dishes, fish or chicken.

SERVES FOUR

350g/12oz/generous 1¾ cups
    long grain rice
60ml/4 tbsp groundnut (peanut) oil
1 small onion, finely chopped
2 green chillies, seeded and finely chopped
25g/1oz garlic chives, chopped
15g/½oz fresh coriander (cilantro)
600ml/1 pint/2½ cups vegetable or
    mushroom stock
2.5ml/½ tsp sea salt
250g/9oz mixed mushrooms, thickly sliced
50g/2oz cashew nuts, fried in 15ml/1 tbsp
    olive oil until golden brown
ground black pepper

1 Wash and drain the rice. Heat half the oil in a pan and cook the onion and chillies over a gentle heat, stirring occasionally, for 10–12 minutes until soft.

2 Set half the garlic chives aside. Cut the stalks off the coriander and set the leaves aside. Purée the remaining chives and the coriander stalks with the stock in a food processor or blender.

VARIATION

For a higher-fibre alternative make this dish with brown rice. Increase the cooking time in step 3 to 25–30 minutes or follow the packet instructions.

3 Add the rice to the onions and fry over a low heat, stirring frequently, for 4–5 minutes. Pour in the stock mixture, then stir in the salt and a good grinding of black pepper. Bring to the boil, then stir and reduce the heat to very low. Cover tightly with a lid and cook for 15–20 minutes, or until the rice has absorbed all the liquid.

4 Remove the pan from the heat and lay a clean, folded dishtowel over the pan, under the lid, and press on the lid to wedge it firmly in place. Leave the rice to stand for a further 10 minutes, allowing the towel to absorb the steam while the rice becomes completely tender.

5 Meanwhile, heat the remaining oil in a frying pan and cook the mushrooms for 5–6 minutes until tender and browned. Add the remaining garlic chives and cook for another 1–2 minutes.

6 Stir the cooked mushroom and chive mixture and chopped coriander leaves into the rice. Adjust the seasoning to taste, then transfer to a warmed serving dish and serve immediately, sprinkled with the fried cashew nuts.

ROASTED SHALLOT and SQUASH SALAD

This is especially good served with a grain or starchy salad, based on rice or couscous, for example. Serve with plenty of home-made organic bread to mop up the juices.

SERVES FOUR TO SIX

75ml/5 tbsp olive oil

15ml/1 tbsp balsamic vinegar, plus a little extra, if you like

15ml/1 tbsp sweet soy sauce

350g/12oz shallots, peeled but left whole

3 fresh red chillies

1 butternut squash, peeled, seeded and cut into chunks

5ml/1 tsp finely chopped fresh thyme

15g/½oz flat leaf parsley

1 small garlic clove, finely chopped

75g/3oz/¾ cup walnuts, chopped

150g/5oz feta cheese

sea salt and ground black pepper

1 Preheat the oven to 200°C/400°F/ Gas 6. Beat the olive oil, balsamic vinegar and soy sauce together in a large bowl, then season with a little salt and plenty of freshly ground black pepper.

2 Toss the shallots and two of the chillies in the oil mixture and add to a large roasting pan or ovenproof dish. Roast for 15 minutes, stirring once or twice.

3 Add the butternut squash chunks and roast for a further 30–35 minutes, stirring once, until the squash is tender and browned. Remove from the oven, stir in the chopped fresh thyme and set the vegetables aside to cool.

4 Chop the parsley and garlic together and mix with the walnuts. Seed and finely chop the remaining chilli.

5 Stir the parsley, garlic and walnut mixture into the vegetables. Add chopped chilli to taste and adjust the seasoning, adding a little extra balsamic vinegar, if you like. Crumble the feta and add it to the salad. Transfer to a serving dish and serve immediately.

POTATOES and PARSNIPS BAKED with GARLIC and CREAM

As the potatoes and parsnips cook, they gradually absorb the garlic-flavoured cream, while the cheese browns to a crispy finish.

SERVES FOUR TO SIX

3 large potatoes, total weight
    about 675g/1½lb
350g/12oz small–medium parsnips
200ml/7fl oz/scant 1 cup single (light)
    cream or soya cream
105ml/7 tbsp milk or soya milk
2 garlic cloves, crushed
butter or olive oil, for greasing
about 5ml/1 tsp freshly grated
    nutmeg
75g/3oz/¾ cup coarsely grated
    Cheddar cheese
sea salt and ground black pepper

3 Lightly grease a 25cm/10in long, shallow rectangular earthenware baking dish with butter or oil. Preheat the oven to 180°C/350°F/Gas 4.

5 Pour the garlic-flavoured cream and milk mixture into the dish and then press the sliced potatoes and parsnips down into the liquid. The liquid should come to just underneath the top layer of vegetables. Cover the dish with a piece of lightly buttered foil or baking parchment and bake for 45 minutes.

1 Peel the potatoes and parsnips and cut them into thin slices using a sharp knife. Place them in a steamer and cook for 5 minutes. Leave to cool slightly.

4 Arrange the thinly sliced potatoes and parsnips in layers in the greased earthenware dish, sprinkling each layer of vegetables with a little freshly grated nutmeg, a little salt and plenty of ground black pepper.

6 Remove the dish from the oven and remove the foil or paper from the dish. Sprinkle the grated Cheddar cheese over the vegetables in an even layer.

7 Return the dish to the oven and bake uncovered for a further 20–30 minutes, or until the potatoes and parsnips are tender and the topping is golden brown.

COOK'S TIPS
• If you have one, use a mandolin or a food processor fitted with a slicing blade to slice the potatoes and parsnips thinly and evenly for this gratin.
• At the end of the cooking time, to test if the vegetables are tender, insert a sharp knife through the middle of the potatoes and parsnips. The knife should slide in easily and the vegetables feel soft.

2 Meanwhile, pour the cream and milk into a heavy pan, add the crushed garlic and bring to the boil over a medium heat. Remove the pan from the heat and leave to stand at room temperature for about 10 minutes to allow the flavour of the garlic to infuse into the cream and milk mixture.

VARIATIONS
• Use sweet potatoes in place of some or all of the ordinary potatoes – choose orange-fleshed ones for a pretty colour contrast with the parsnips. Other root vegetables such as Jerusalem artichokes, carrots, swede (rutabaga) or turnips would also work well.
• Other hard cheeses would be equally good in this recipe – try Red Leicester or Gruyère, or go for the even more strongly flavoured Parmesan, premium Italian-style vegetarian cheese or Pecorino.

DUCK SAUSAGES with SPICY PLUM SAUCE

A variety of organic sausages are available direct from farmer's markets and small butchers, and any pork or game sausages would work in this dish. Rich duck sausages are best baked.

SERVES FOUR

8–12 duck sausages

For the sweet potato mash
1.5kg/3¼lb sweet potatoes
25g/1oz/2 tbsp butter or
    30ml/2 tbsp olive oil
60ml/4 tbsp milk
sea salt and ground black pepper

For the plum sauce
30ml/2 tbsp olive oil
1 small onion, chopped
1 small red chilli, seeded and chopped
450g/1lb plums, stoned (pitted)
    and chopped
30ml/2 tbsp red wine vinegar
45ml/3 tbsp clear honey

1 Preheat the oven to 190°C/375°F/ Gas 5. Arrange the duck sausages in a single layer in a large, shallow ovenproof dish. Bake the sausages, uncovered, in the oven for 25–30 minutes, turning the sausages two or three times during cooking, to ensure that they brown and cook evenly.

2 Cut the sweet potatoes into chunks, put in a pan and add boiling water to cover. Simmer for 20 minutes, or until tender.

3 Drain and mash the potatoes, then place the pan over a low heat. Stir frequently for about 5 minutes to dry out the mashed potato. Beat in the butter or oil and milk, season to taste.

4 Make the plum sauce. Heat the oil in a small pan and fry the onion and chilli gently for 5 minutes. Stir in the plums, vinegar and honey, then simmer gently for 10 minutes.

5 Serve the freshly cooked sausages with the sweet potato mash and plum sauce.

SPICY VENISON CASSEROLE

Being high in flavour but low in saturated fat, organic venison is a good choice for healthy, yet rich, casseroles. Cranberries and orange bring a delicious fruitiness to this spicy recipe.

SERVES FOUR

15ml/1 tbsp olive oil
1 onion, chopped
2 celery sticks, sliced
10ml/2 tsp ground allspice
15ml/1 tbsp plain (all-purpose) or
    wholemeal (whole-wheat) flour
675g/1½lb stewing venison, diced
225g/8oz fresh or frozen cranberries
grated rind and juice of 1 orange
900ml/1½ pints/3¾ cups beef or
    venison stock
sea salt and ground black pepper

1 Heat the oil in a flameproof casserole. Add the onion and celery and fry for about 5 minutes, or until softened.

2 Meanwhile, mix the ground allspice with the flour and either spread the mixture out on a large plate or place in a large plastic bag. Toss a few pieces of venison at a time (to prevent them becoming soggy) in the flour mixture until they are all lightly coated. Spread the floured venison out on a large plate until ready to cook.

3 When the onion and celery are just softened, remove them from the casserole using a slotted spoon and set aside. Add the venison pieces to the casserole in batches and cook until well browned and sealed on all sides.

COOK'S TIP
Freshly made home-made stock is always best, but if you are short of time, look for cartons or tubs of fresh stock in the chilled food cabinets of organic stores.

4 Add the cranberries and the orange rind and juice to the casserole along with the stock and stir well. Return the vegetables and the browned venison to the casserole and heat until simmering. Cover tightly and reduce the heat.

5 Simmer for about 45 minutes, or until the venison is tender, stirring occasionally. Season the venison casserole to taste with a little salt and plenty of ground black pepper before serving.

VARIATIONS
Farmed organic venison is increasingly easy to find and is available from many good butchers and organic meat delivery companies. It makes a rich and flavourful stew, but lean pork or braising steak could be used in place of the venison, if you prefer. You could also replace the cranberries with pitted and halved prunes and, for extra flavour, use either ale or stout instead of about half the stock.

SOLE with WILD MUSHROOMS

Try to use chanterelle mushrooms for this delicious fish dish; their glowing orange colour combines wonderfully with the intensely golden sauce.

SERVES FOUR

4 Dover sole fillets, about 115g/4oz
   each, skinned
50g/2oz/¼ cup butter or
   non-hydrogenated margarine
500ml/17fl oz/generous 2 cups fish stock
150g/5oz/2 cups chanterelles or
   oyster mushrooms
a large pinch of saffron threads
150ml/¼ pint/⅔ cup double (heavy) cream
   or soya cream
1 egg yolk
sea salt and ground white pepper
flat leaf parsley sprigs, to garnish
boiled new potatoes and steamed broccoli
   florets, to serve

1 Preheat the oven to 200°C/400°F/
Gas 6.

2 Cut the sole fillets in half lengthways and place them on a board with the skinned side uppermost. Season, then roll them up.

3 Use a little of the butter to grease a baking dish just large enough to hold all the sole fillets in a single layer. Arrange the rolls in it, then pour over the fish stock.

4 Cover tightly with foil and bake for 12–15 minutes until cooked through.

5 Meanwhile, pick off any bits of fern or twig from the mushrooms and wipe the mushrooms with a damp cloth. Halve or quarter any large ones.

6 Heat the remaining butter in a frying pan until foaming and sauté the mushrooms for 3–4 minutes until just tender. Season with salt and pepper and keep hot.

7 Lift the cooked sole fillets out of the cooking liquid and place them on a heated serving dish. Keep hot.

8 Strain the liquid into a small pan, add the saffron, set over a very high heat and boil until reduced to about 250ml/8fl oz/1 cup.

9 Stir in the cream and let the sauce bubble gently for a few seconds.

10 Lightly beat the egg yolk in a small bowl, pour on a little of the hot sauce and stir well. Add the mixture to the remaining sauce in the pan and cook over a very low heat for 1–2 minutes until slightly thickened. Season to taste with plenty of salt and pepper.

11 Stir the mushrooms into the sauce and pour it over the sole fillets.

12 Garnish with parsley sprigs and serve immediately. Boiled new potatoes and steamed broccoli florets make the perfect accompaniment.

POTATO-TOPPED FISH PIE

This traditional Scottish dish should be prepared from wild fish such as hoki, caught sustainably. Always ensure you buy wild fish bearing the MSC logo.

SERVES FOUR

675g/1½lb hoki fillets (or other sustainably
    caught white fish)
300ml/½ pint/1¼ cups milk or soya milk
½ lemon, sliced
1 bay leaf
1 fresh thyme sprig
4–5 black peppercorns
50g/2oz/¼ cup butter or
    non-hydrogenated margarine
25g/1oz/¼ cup plain (all-purpose) flour
30ml/2 tbsp chopped fresh parsley
5ml/1 tsp anchovy essence
150g/5oz/2 cups shiitake or brown cap
    (cremini) mushrooms, sliced
sea salt, ground black pepper and
    cayenne pepper

For the topping

450g/1lb potatoes, cooked and mashed
    with milk or soya milk
50g/2oz/¼ cup butter or
    non-hydrogenated margarine
2 tomatoes, sliced
25g/1oz/¼ cup grated Cheddar cheese

1 Put the fish skin side down in a shallow pan. Add the milk, lemon slices, bay leaf, thyme and peppercorns. Bring to the boil, then lower the heat and poach gently for about 5 minutes until just cooked. Strain off and reserve the milk. Remove the fish skin and flake the flesh, discarding any bones.

2 Melt half the butter in a small pan, stir in the flour and cook gently for 1 minute. Add the reserved milk and boil, whisking, until smooth and creamy. Stir in the parsley and anchovy essence and season to taste.

3 Heat the remaining butter in a frying pan, add the sliced mushrooms and sauté until tender. Season and add to the flaked fish. Mix the sauce into the fish and stir gently to combine. Transfer the mixture to an ovenproof casserole.

4 Preheat the oven to 200°C/400°F/ Gas 6. Beat the mashed potato with the butter until very creamy. Season, then spread the topping evenly over the fish. Fork up the surface and arrange the sliced tomatoes around the edge. Sprinkle the exposed topping with the grated cheese.

5 Bake for 20–25 minutes until the topping is browned. If you prefer, finish the browning under a hot grill (broiler).

VARIATION
Instead of using plain mashed potatoes, try a mixture of mashed potato and mashed swede (rutabaga) or sweet potato.

STICKY PEAR PUDDING

Pears are at their best in autumn and, combined with other organic ingredients such as cloves, coffee and maple syrup, they form the basis of this indulgent dessert.

SERVES SIX

30ml/2 tbsp ground coffee
15ml/1 tbsp near-boiling water
4 ripe pears
juice of ½ orange
50g/2oz/½ cup toasted hazelnuts
115g/4oz/½ cup butter or
   non-hydrogenated margarine, softened
115g/4oz/generous ½ cup unrefined caster
   (superfine) sugar, plus an extra
   15ml/1 tbsp for baking
2 eggs, beaten
50g/2oz/½ cup self-raising (self-rising)
   flour, sifted
pinch of ground cloves
8 whole cloves (optional)
45ml/3 tbsp maple syrup
fine strips of orange rind, to decorate

For the orange cream
300ml/½ pint/1¼ cups whipping cream
15ml/1 tbsp unrefined icing
   (confectioners') sugar, sifted
finely grated rind of ½ orange

1 Preheat the oven to 180°C/350°F/ Gas 4. Lightly grease a 20cm/8in loose-based sandwich tin (shallow cake pan).

2 Put the ground coffee in a small bowl and pour the water over. Leave to infuse (steep) for 4 minutes, then strain through a fine sieve (strainer).

VARIATION

Apple and cinnamon could be used in this pudding instead of pears and cloves, with a lemon cream in place of orange cream.

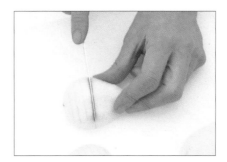

3 Peel, halve and core the pears. Thinly slice across the pear halves part of the way through. Brush the pears with orange juice. Grind the hazelnuts in a coffee grinder until fine.

4 Beat the butter and the caster sugar together until very light and fluffy. Gradually beat in the eggs, then fold in the flour, ground cloves, hazelnuts and coffee.

5 Spoon the mixture into the prepared sandwich tin and level the surface with a spatula.

6 Pat the pears dry on kitchen paper, then arrange them carefully in the sponge mixture, flat side down.

7 Lightly press two whole cloves, if using, into each pear half. Brush the pears with 15ml/1 tbsp maple syrup.

8 Sprinkle 15ml/1 tbsp caster sugar over the pears. Bake for 45–50 minutes, or until firm and well risen.

9 While the sponge is cooking, make the orange cream. Whip the cream, icing sugar and orange rind until soft peaks form. Spoon into a serving dish and chill until needed.

10 Allow the sponge to cool for about 10 minutes in the tin, then remove and place on a serving plate. Lightly brush with the remaining maple syrup before decorating with orange rind. Serve warm with the orange cream.

COOK'S TIP

Organic pears are a good source of soluble fibre and are great at lowering cholesterol and easing constipation. Buy slightly underripe fruit and leave them to ripen on a sunny windowsill for a few days – overripe pears go off quickly.

BAKED APPLE DUMPLINGS

A wonderful way to make the most of apples in season. The sharpness of the fruit contrasts perfectly with the maple syrup drizzled over this delightful pastry parcel.

SERVES EIGHT

8 firm cooking apples, peeled
1 egg white
130g/4½oz/⅔ cup unrefined caster
    (superfine) sugar
45ml/3 tbsp double (heavy) cream or
    soya cream, plus extra whipped cream,
    to serve
2.5ml/½ tsp vanilla essence (extract)
250ml/8fl oz/1 cup maple syrup

For the pastry
475g/1lb 2oz/4½ cups plain
    (all-purpose) flour
350g/12oz/1½ cups butter or
    non-hydrogenated margarine, diced

1 To make the pastry, sift the flour into a large bowl. Rub in the butter until the mixture resembles fine breadcrumbs.

2 Sprinkle over 175ml/6fl oz/¾ cup water and mix until the dough holds together, adding more water if necessary. Gather into a ball. Wrap in clear film (plastic wrap) and chill for 10 minutes. Preheat the oven to 220°C/425°F/Gas 7.

3 Cutting from the stem end, core the apples without cutting through the base. Roll out the pastry thinly. Cut squares almost large enough to enclose the apples; brush with egg white and set an apple in the centre of each.

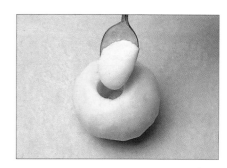

4 Cut pastry rounds to cover the tops of the cored apples. Reserve the pastry trimmings. Combine the unrefined sugar, cream and vanilla essence in a small bowl. Spoon one-eighth of the mixture into the hollow of each apple.

5 Place a pastry round on top of each apple, then bring up the sides of the pastry square to enclose it, pleating the larger piece of pastry to make a snug fit around the apple. Moisten the joins with cold water where they overlap and press down so they stick in place.

6 Make apple stalks and leaves from the pastry trimmings and use to decorate the dumplings. Set them in a large greased baking dish, at least 2cm/¾in apart. Bake for 30 minutes, then reduce the oven temperature to 180°C/350°F/Gas 4 and continue baking for 20 minutes more, or until the pastry is golden brown and the apples are tender.

7 Transfer the dumplings to a serving dish. Mix the maple syrup with the juices in the baking dish and drizzle over the dumplings. Serve the dumplings hot with whipped cream.

HOT BLACKBERRY and APPLE SOUFFLÉS

The deliciously tart autumn flavours of blackberry and apple complement each other perfectly to make a light, mouthwatering hot pudding.

MAKES SIX

butter or non-hydrogenated margarine,
    for greasing
150g/5oz/¾ cup unrefined caster (superfine)
    sugar, plus extra for dusting
350g/12oz/3 cups blackberries
1 large cooking apple, peeled and finely diced
grated rind and juice of 1 orange
3 egg whites
unrefined icing (confectioners') sugar,
    for dusting

1 Preheat the oven to 200°C/400°F/
Gas 6. Generously grease six 150ml/
¼ pint/⅔ cup individual soufflé dishes
with butter and dust with caster sugar,
shaking out the excess sugar.

2 Put a baking sheet in the oven to heat.
Cook the blackberries, diced apple and
orange rind and juice in a pan for
10 minutes or until the apple has pulped
down well. Press through a sieve
(strainer) into a bowl. Stir in 50g/2oz/¼
cup of the caster sugar. Set aside to cool.

3 Put a spoonful of the fruit purée into
each prepared soufflé dish and spread
evenly. Set the dishes aside.

4 Place the egg whites in a grease-free
bowl and whisk until they form stiff
peaks. Very gradually whisk in the
remaining caster sugar to make a stiff,
glossy meringue mixture.

5 Fold in the remaining fruit purée and
spoon the flavoured meringue into the
prepared dishes. Level the tops with a
metal spatula, and run a table knife
around the edge of each dish.

6 Place the dishes on the hot baking
sheet and bake for 10–15 minutes until
the soufflés have risen well and are
lightly browned. Dust the tops with
icing sugar and serve immediately.

COOK'S TIP
Running a table knife around the inside
edge of the soufflé dishes before baking
helps the soufflés to rise evenly without
sticking to the rim of the dish.

OAT and RAISIN DROP SCONES

*Serve these easy-to-make organic scones at tea time or as a dessert – or even
a special breakfast or brunch – with real maple syrup or clear honey.*

MAKES ABOUT SIXTEEN

75g/3oz/⅔ cup self-raising (self-rising) flour
2.5ml/½ tsp baking powder
50g/2oz/scant ½ cup raisins
25g/1oz/¼ cup fine oatmeal
25g/1oz/2 tbsp unrefined caster
   (superfine) sugar
grated rind of 1 orange
2 egg yolks
10g/¼oz/½ tbsp unsalted butter or non-
   hydrogenated margarine, melted
200ml/7fl oz/scant 1 cup single (light)
   cream or soya cream
200ml/7fl oz/scant 1 cup water
sunflower oil, for greasing
icing (confectioners') sugar, for dusting

1 Sift the self-raising flour and baking
powder together into a large mixing bowl.

COOK'S TIP
Wrap the cooked scones in a clean dish
towel to keep them soft.

2 Add the raisins, oatmeal, sugar and
orange rind. Gradually beat in the egg
yolks, butter, cream and water to make
a creamy batter.

3 Lightly grease and heat a large heavy
frying pan or griddle and drop about
30ml/2 tbsp of batter at a time on to
the pan or griddle to make six or seven
small pancakes.

4 Cook over a moderate heat until
bubbles show on the scones' surface,
then turn them over and cook for a
further 2 minutes until golden.

5 Transfer to a plate and dust with icing
sugar. Keep warm while cooking the
remaining mixture. Serve warm.

PARSNIP CAKE with ORANGE ICING

This fabulous vegan cake is similar to the ever-popular carrot cake, but uses non-dairy alternatives to margarine and cream cheese.

SERVES TEN

250g/9oz/2¼ cups wholemeal (whole-wheat) self-raising (self-rising) flour
15ml/1 tbsp baking powder
5ml/1 tsp ground cinnamon
5ml/1 tsp freshly ground nutmeg
130g/4½oz/9 tbsp vegan margarine
130g/4½oz/scant ½ cup unrefined soft light brown sugar
250g/9oz parsnips, coarsely grated
1 banana, mashed
finely grated rind and juice of 1 orange

For the topping
225g/8oz/1 cup organic soya cream cheese
45ml/3 tbsp unrefined icing (confectioners') sugar
juice of 1 small orange
fine strips of orange peel

1 Preheat the oven to 180°C/350°F/Gas 4. Lightly grease and line the base of a 900g/2lb loaf tin (pan).

2 Sift the flour, baking powder and spices into a large bowl. Add any bran remaining in the sieve (strainer).

COOK'S TIP
If you can't find self-raising wholemeal flour, use ordinary wholemeal flour and add an extra 15ml/1 tbsp baking powder.

VARIATION
Serve the cake as a dessert with a generous spoonful of organic natural (plain) yogurt, crème fraîche or soya cream, flavoured with grated orange rind or a little Calvados.

3 Melt the margarine in a pan, add the sugar and stir until dissolved. Make a well in the flour mixture, then add the melted margarine and sugar. Mix in the parsnips, banana and orange rind and juice. Spoon the mixture into the prepared tin and level the top with the back of a spoon.

4 Bake for 45–50 minutes until a skewer inserted into the centre of the cake comes out clean. Allow the cake to cool slightly before removing from the tin, then transfer to a wire rack to cool completely.

5 To make the topping, beat together the cream cheese, icing sugar, orange juice and strips of orange peel until smooth. Spread the topping evenly over the cake.

WINTER

Warming comfort food is the order of the day in cold weather to help keep out winter chills. Root vegetables such as carrots, turnips and parsnips are readily available and can be included in winter soups, stews and casseroles such as Chicken Casserole with Winter Vegetables, or Braised Shoulder of Mutton with Pearl Barley and Baby Vegetables. For vegetarians, substantial main courses include warming ingredients such as pulses, grains and spices – try Parsnips and Chickpeas in Garlic, Onion, Chilli and Ginger Paste, or Barley Risotto with Roasted Squash and Leeks. Rich, meaty dishes to enjoy during the coldest months of the year include Chilli con Carne and Boeuf Bourguignonne – delicious served with mashed root vegetables and organic red wine. Fish dishes for the winter season are best served with the addition of well-flavoured ingredients: try Fillets of Brill in Red Wine Sauce, or Smoked Haddock with Mustard Cabbage. Sweet winter treats to enjoy include Baked Maple and Pecan Croissant Pudding, and Orange Marmalade Chocolate Loaf.

PARSNIPS and CHICKPEAS in GARLIC, ONION, CHILLI and GINGER PASTE

Organic root vegetables, such as parsnips, often have a knobbly appearance that makes them interesting and individual, and their flavours are sweeter and more intense.

SERVES FOUR

200g/7oz/1 cup dried chickpeas, soaked
   overnight in cold water, then drained
7 garlic cloves, finely chopped
1 small onion, chopped
5cm/2in piece fresh root ginger, chopped
2 green chillies, seeded and finely chopped
450ml/¾ pint/scant 2 cups plus
   75ml/5 tbsp water
60ml/4 tbsp sunflower oil
5ml/1 tsp cumin seeds
10ml/2 tsp ground coriander seeds
5ml/1 tsp ground turmeric
2.5–5ml/½–1 tsp chilli powder
   or mild paprika
50g/2oz/½ cup cashew nuts, toasted
   and ground
250g/9oz tomatoes, peeled and chopped
900g/2lb parsnips, cut into chunks
5ml/1 tsp ground roasted cumin seeds
juice of 1 lime, to taste
sea salt and ground black pepper

To serve
fresh coriander (cilantro) leaves
a few cashew nuts, toasted
natural (plain) yogurt
naan bread or chapatis

1 Put the soaked chickpeas in a pan, cover with cold water and bring to the boil. Boil vigorously for 10 minutes, then reduce the heat so that the water boils steadily. Cook for 1–1½ hours, or until the chickpeas are tender. (The cooking time depends on how long the chickpeas have been stored.) Drain and set aside.

2 Set 10ml/2 tsp of the finely chopped garlic aside, then place the remainder in a food processor or blender with the onion, ginger and half the chopped chillies. Add the 75ml/5 tbsp water and process to make a smooth paste.

COOK'S TIP
Do not add salt to the water when cooking dried chickpeas, as this will toughen them.

3 Heat the oil in a frying pan and cook the cumin seeds for 30 seconds. Stir in the coriander seeds, turmeric, chilli powder or paprika and the ground cashew nuts. Add the ginger paste and cook, stirring frequently, until the water begins to evaporate. Add the tomatoes and stir-fry for 2–3 minutes.

4 Mix in the cooked chickpeas and parsnip chunks with the 450ml/¾ pint/ scant 2 cups water, a little salt and plenty of black pepper. Bring to the boil, stir, then simmer, uncovered, for 15–20 minutes until the parsnips are completely tender.

5 Reduce the liquid, if necessary, by bringing the sauce to the boil and then boiling fiercely until the sauce is thick. Add the ground roasted cumin with more salt and/or lime juice to taste. Stir in the reserved garlic and green chilli, and cook for a further 1–2 minutes. Sprinkle the fresh coriander leaves and toasted cashew nuts over and serve straight away with yogurt and warmed naan bread or chapatis.

BARLEY RISOTTO with ROASTED SQUASH and LEEKS

This is more like a pilaff, made with slightly chewy, nutty-flavoured pearl barley, than a classic risotto. Sweet organic leeks and roasted squash are superb with this earthy grain.

SERVES FOUR TO FIVE

200g/7oz/1 cup pearl barley
1 butternut squash, peeled, seeded and
    cut into chunks
10ml/2 tsp chopped fresh thyme
60ml/4 tbsp olive oil
25g/1oz/2 tbsp butter
4 leeks, cut into fairly thick diagonal slices
2 garlic cloves, finely chopped
175g/6oz/2½ cups brown cap (cremini)
    mushrooms, sliced
2 carrots, coarsely grated
about 120ml/4fl oz/½ cup vegetable stock
30ml/2 tbsp chopped fresh flat leaf parsley
50g/2oz/⅔ cup Parmesan cheese, grated
    or shaved
45ml/3 tbsp pumpkin seeds, toasted, or
    chopped walnuts
sea salt and ground black pepper

1 Rinse the barley, then cook it in simmering water, keeping the pan part-covered, for 35–45 minutes, or until tender. Drain. Preheat the oven to 200°C/400°F/Gas 6.

2 Place the squash in a roasting pan with half the thyme. Season with pepper and toss with half the oil. Roast, stirring once, for 30–35 minutes, until the squash is tender and beginning to brown.

3 Heat half the butter with the remaining olive oil in a large frying pan. Cook the leeks and garlic gently for 5 minutes. Add the mushrooms and remaining thyme, then cook until the liquid from the mushrooms evaporates and they begin to fry.

4 Stir in the carrots and cook for about 2 minutes, then add the barley and most of the vegetable stock. Season well and part-cover the pan. Cook for a further 5 minutes. Pour in the remaining stock if the mixture seems dry.

5 Stir in the parsley, the remaining butter and half the cheese, then stir in the squash. Add seasoning to taste and serve immediately, sprinkled with the toasted pumpkin seeds or walnuts and the remaining cheese.

VARIATIONS

• Make the risotto with organic brown rice instead of the barley – cook following the packet instructions and continue from step 2.
• Any type of organic mushrooms can be used in this recipe – try sliced field (portabello) mushrooms for a hearty flavour.

PEPPERS FILLED with SPICED VEGETABLES

Indian spices season the potato and aubergine stuffing in these colourful baked peppers.
They are good with brown rice and a lentil dhal. Alternatively, serve them with a salad,
Indian breads and a cucumber or mint and yogurt raita.

SERVES SIX

6 large evenly shaped red or
   yellow (bell) peppers
500g/1¼lb waxy potatoes
1 small onion, chopped
4–5 garlic cloves, chopped
5cm/2in piece fresh root ginger, chopped
1–2 fresh green chillies, seeded
   and chopped
105ml/7 tbsp water
90–105ml/6–7 tbsp sunflower oil
1 aubergine (eggplant), diced
10ml/2 tsp cumin seeds
5ml/1 tsp kalonji seeds
2.5ml/½ tsp ground turmeric
5ml/1 tsp ground coriander
5ml/1 tsp ground toasted cumin seeds
pinch of cayenne pepper
about 30ml/2 tbsp lemon juice
sea salt and ground black pepper
30ml/2 tbsp chopped fresh coriander
   (cilantro), to garnish

1 Cut the tops off the red or yellow peppers, then remove and discard the seeds. Cut a thin slice off the base of the peppers, if necessary, to make them stand upright.

2 Bring a large pan of lightly salted water to the boil. Add the peppers and cook for 5–6 minutes. Drain and leave them upside down in a colander.

COOK'S TIP
The hottest part of a chilli is the white membrane that connects the seeds to the flesh. Removing the seeds and membrane before cooking gives a milder flavour.

3 Cook the potatoes in lightly salted, boiling water for 10–12 minutes until just tender. Drain, cool and peel, then cut into 1cm/½in dice.

4 Put the onion, garlic, ginger and green chillies in a food processor or blender with 60ml/4 tbsp of the water and process to a purée.

5 Heat 45ml/3 tbsp of the sunflower oil in a large, deep frying pan and cook the diced aubergine, stirring occasionally, until it is evenly browned on all sides. Remove from the pan and set aside. Add another 30ml/2 tbsp of the sunflower oil to the pan, add the diced potatoes and cook until lightly browned on all sides. Remove the potatoes from the pan and set aside.

6 If necessary, add another 15ml/1 tbsp sunflower oil to the pan, then add the cumin and kalonji seeds. Fry briefly until the seeds darken, then add the turmeric, coriander and ground cumin. Cook for 15 seconds. Stir in the onion and garlic purée and fry, scraping the pan with a spatula, until the onions begin to brown.

7 Return the potatoes and aubergine to the pan, season with salt, pepper and 1–2 pinches of cayenne. Add the remaining water and 15ml/1 tbsp lemon juice and then cook, stirring, until the liquid evaporates. Preheat the oven to 190°C/375°F/Gas 5.

8 Fill the peppers with the spiced vegetable mixture and place on a lightly greased baking tray. Brush the peppers with a little oil and bake for 30–35 minutes until they are cooked. Allow to cool a little, then sprinkle with a little more lemon juice, garnish with the coriander and serve.

COOK'S TIP
Kalonji, or nigella as it is also known, is a tiny black seed. It is widely used in Indian cooking, especially sprinkled over breads or in potato dishes. It has a mild, slightly nutty flavour and is best toasted for a few seconds in a dry or lightly oiled frying pan over a medium heat before using in a recipe. This helps to bring out its flavour, as with most spices.

CHICKEN CASSEROLE with WINTER VEGETABLES

A casserole of wonderfully tender organic chicken, winter root vegetables and lentils, finished with crème fraîche, mustard and tarragon.

SERVES FOUR

350g/12oz onions
350g/12oz leeks
225g/8oz carrots
450g/1lb swede (rutabaga)
30ml/2 tbsp olive oil
4 chicken portions, about 900g/2lb
    total weight
115g/4oz/½ cup green lentils
475ml/16fl oz/2 cups chicken stock
300ml/½ pint/1¼ cups apple juice
10ml/2 tsp cornflour (cornstarch)
45ml/3 tbsp crème fraîche
10ml/2 tsp wholegrain mustard
30ml/2 tbsp chopped fresh tarragon
sea salt and ground black pepper
fresh tarragon sprigs, to garnish

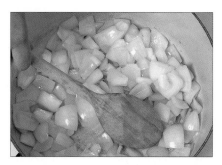

1 Preheat the oven to 190°C/375°F/ Gas 5. Prepare and chop the vegetables.

2 Heat the oil in a large flameproof casserole. Season the chicken portions and brown them in the hot oil until golden. Remove the chicken from the pan.

3 Add the onions to the casserole and cook for 5 minutes, stirring, until they begin to soften and colour. Add the leeks, carrots, swede and lentils to the casserole and stir over a medium heat for 2 minutes.

4 Return the chicken to the pan, then add the stock, apple juice and seasoning. Bring to the boil and cover tightly. Cook in the oven for 50–60 minutes, or until the chicken and lentils are tender.

5 Place the casserole on the hob (stovetop) over a medium heat. In a small bowl, blend the cornflour with about 30ml/2 tbsp water to make a smooth paste and add to the casserole with the crème fraîche, wholegrain mustard and chopped tarragon. Adjust the seasoning, then simmer gently for about 2 minutes, stirring, until thickened slightly, before serving, garnished with tarragon sprigs.

COOK'S TIP
Chop the vegetables into similarly sized pieces so that they cook evenly. Organic vegetables do not need to be peeled.

BRAISED SHOULDER of MUTTON with PEARL BARLEY and BABY VEGETABLES

A wonderful variety of organic grains is readily available. In this tasty winter stew, pearl barley absorbs all the juices to become full-flavoured with a nutty texture when cooked.

SERVES FOUR

60ml/4 tbsp olive oil

1 large onion, chopped

2 garlic cloves, chopped

2 celery sticks, sliced

a little plain (all-purpose) or wholemeal (whole-wheat) flour

675g/1½lb boned shoulder of mutton, cut into cubes

900ml–1 litre/1½–1¾ pints/3¾–4 cups mutton stock

115g/4oz/½ cup pearl barley

225g/8oz baby carrots

225g/8oz baby turnips

sea salt and ground black pepper

30ml/2 tbsp chopped fresh marjoram, to garnish

warm, crusty bread, to serve

1 Heat 45ml/3 tbsp of the oil in a flameproof casserole. Cook the onion and garlic until softened, add the celery, then cook until the vegetables brown.

2 Season the flour and toss the mutton in it. Use a draining spoon to remove the vegetables from the casserole. Add the remaining oil to the juices in the casserole and heat. Brown the mutton in batches until golden.

3 When all the meat is browned, return it to the casserole with the vegetables. Stir in 900ml/1½ pints/3¾ cups of the stock and the pearl barley. Cover, then bring to the boil, reduce the heat and simmer for 1 hour, or until the pearl barley and mutton are tender.

4 Add the baby carrots and turnips to the casserole for the final 15 minutes of cooking. Stir the meat occasionally during cooking and add the remaining stock, if necessary. Stir in seasoning to taste, and serve piping hot, garnished with marjoram, with warm, crusty bread as an accompaniment.

BOEUF BOURGUIGNONNE

This classic French dish of beef cooked in Burgundy style, with red wine, small pieces of bacon, baby onions and mushrooms, is traditionally cooked for several hours at a low temperature. Using organic top rump or braising steak reduces the cooking time.

SERVES SIX

175g/6oz rindless streaky (fatty) bacon rashers (strips), chopped
900g/2lb lean braising steak, such as top rump of beef or braising steak
30ml/2 tbsp plain (all-purpose) or wholemeal (whole-wheat) flour
45ml/3 tbsp sunflower oil
25g/1oz/2 tbsp butter or 30ml/2 tbsp olive oil
12 shallots
2 garlic cloves, crushed
175g/6oz/2½ cups mushrooms, sliced
450ml/¾ pint/scant 2 cups robust red wine
150ml/¼ pint/⅔ cup beef stock or consommé
1 bay leaf
2 sprigs each of fresh thyme, parsley and marjoram
sea salt and ground black pepper
mashed root vegetables, such as celeriac and potatoes, to serve

1 Preheat the oven to 160°C/325°F/Gas 3. Heat a large flameproof casserole, then add the bacon and cook, stirring occasionally, until the pieces are crisp and golden brown.

2 Meanwhile, cut the meat into 2.5cm/1in cubes. Season the flour and use to coat the meat. Use a draining spoon to remove the bacon from the casserole and set aside. Add and heat the sunflower oil, then brown the beef in batches and set aside with the bacon.

COOK'S TIP
Boeuf Bourguignonne freezes very well. Freeze for up to 2 months. Thaw overnight in the refrigerator, then transfer to a flameproof casserole and add 150ml/¼ pint/⅔ cup water. Stir well, bring to the boil, stirring occasionally, and simmer steadily for at least 10 minutes, or until the meat is piping hot.

3 Add the butter or olive oil to the casserole. Cook the shallots and garlic until just starting to colour, then add the mushrooms and cook for 5 minutes. Replace the bacon and meat, and stir in the wine and stock or consommé. Tie the herbs together and add to the casserole.

4 Cover and cook for 1½ hours, or until the meat is tender, stirring once or twice. Season to taste before serving with mashed root vegetables.

CHILLI CON CARNE

Originally made with finely chopped beef, chillies and kidney beans by hungry labourers working on the Texan railroad, this famous Tex-Mex stew has become an international favourite. Be authentic by using organic ingredients.

SERVES EIGHT

1.2kg/2½lb lean braising steak
30ml/2 tbsp sunflower oil
1 large onion, chopped
2 garlic cloves, finely chopped
15ml/1 tbsp plain (all-purpose) or
    wholemeal (whole-wheat) flour
300ml/½ pint/1¼ cups red wine
300ml/½ pint/1¼ cups beef stock
30ml/2 tbsp tomato purée (paste)
sea salt and ground black pepper
fresh coriander (cilantro) leaves, to garnish
boiled white or brown rice, to serve

For the beans
30ml/2 tbsp olive oil
1 onion, chopped
1 red chilli, seeded and chopped
2 × 400g/14oz cans red kidney beans,
    drained and rinsed
400g/14oz can chopped tomatoes

For the topping
6 tomatoes, peeled and chopped
1 green chilli, seeded and chopped
30ml/2 tbsp chopped fresh chives
30ml/2 tbsp chopped fresh coriander
150ml/¼ pint/⅔ cup sour cream

1 Cut the meat into thick strips and then cut it crossways into small cubes. Heat the oil in a large, flameproof casserole. Add the chopped onion and garlic, and cook, stirring occasionally, for 5–8 minutes until softened but not coloured. Meanwhile, season the flour with a little salt and plenty of pepper and place it on a plate, then toss a batch of meat in it.

2 Use a draining spoon to remove the onion from the pan, then add the floured beef and cook over a high heat, stirring occasionally with a wooden spoon until browned on all sides. Remove from the pan and set aside, then flour and brown another batch of meat.

3 When the last batch of meat is browned, return the first batches with the onion to the pan. Stir in the wine, stock and tomato purée. Bring to the boil, reduce the heat and simmer for 45 minutes, or until the beef is tender.

4 Meanwhile, to make the beans, heat the olive oil in a frying pan and cook the onion and chilli until softened. Add the kidney beans and tomatoes and simmer gently for 20–25 minutes.

5 Mix the tomatoes, chilli, chives and coriander for the topping. Ladle the meat on to plates, then add the beans and the tomato topping. Top with sour cream and coriander leaves and serve with rice.

STEAK, MUSHROOM and ALE PIE

Organic steak has a great quality and fine texture and flavour – it is delicious in this Anglo-Irish dish. Creamy mashed potatoes or parsley-dressed boiled potatoes and slightly crunchy carrots and green beans or cabbage are perfect accompaniments. For a bar-style meal, French fries and a side salad can be served with the pie.

SERVES FOUR

30ml/2 tbsp olive oil
1 large onion, finely chopped
115g/4oz/1½ cups brown cap (cremini) or
    button (white) mushrooms, halved
900g/2lb lean beef in one piece, such as
    rump or braising steak
30ml/2 tbsp plain (all-purpose) wholemeal
    (whole-wheat) flour
45ml/3 tbsp sunflower oil
300ml/½ pint/1¼ cups stout or brown ale
300ml/½ pint/1¼ cups beef stock
    or consommé
500g/1¼lb puff pastry, thawed if frozen
beaten egg, to glaze
sea salt and ground black pepper
steamed organic vegetables, to serve

1 Heat the olive oil in a large, flameproof casserole, add the onion and cook gently, stirring occasionally, for about 5 minutes, or until it is softened but not coloured. Add the halved mushrooms and continue cooking for a further 5 minutes, stirring occasionally.

2 Meanwhile, trim the meat and cut it into 2.5cm/1in cubes. Season the flour and toss the meat in it.

COOK'S TIP
To make individual pies, divide the filling among four individual pie dishes. Cut the pastry into quarters and cover as above. If the dishes do not have rims, press a narrow strip of pastry around the edge of each dish to seal the lid in place. Cook as above, reducing the cooking time slightly.

3 Use a draining spoon to remove the onion mixture from the casserole and set aside. Add and heat the oil, then brown the steak in batches over a high heat to seal in the juices.

4 Replace the vegetables, then stir in the stout or ale and stock or consommé. Bring to the boil, reduce the heat and simmer for about 1 hour, stirring occasionally, or until the meat is tender. Season to taste and transfer to a 1.5 litre/2½ pint/6¼ cup pie dish. Cover and leave to cool. If you have time, chill the meat filling overnight as this allows the flavour to develop. Preheat the oven to 230°C/450°F/Gas 8.

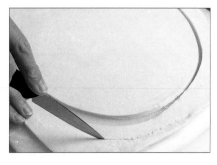

5 Roll out the pastry in the shape of the dish and about 4cm/1½in larger all around. Cut a 2.5cm/1in strip from around the edge of the pastry. Brush the rim of the pie dish with water and press the pastry strip onto it. Brush the pastry rim with beaten egg and cover the pie with the pastry lid. Press the lid firmly in place and then trim the excess pastry from around the edge of the dish.

6 Use the blunt edge of a knife to tap the outside edge of the pastry rim, pressing it down with your finger as you seal the steak and mushroom filling into the dish. (This sealing technique is known as knocking up.)

7 Pinch the outside edge of the pastry between your fingers to flute the edge. Roll out any remaining pastry trimmings and cut out five or six leaf shapes to garnish the centre of the pie. Brush the shapes with a little beaten egg before pressing them lightly in place.

8 Make a hole in the middle of the pie using the point of a sharp knife to allow the steam to escape during cooking. Brush the top carefully with beaten egg and chill for 10 minutes in the refrigerator to rest the pastry.

9 Bake the pie for 15 minutes, then reduce the oven temperature to 200°C/400°F/Gas 6 and bake for a further 15–20 minutes, or until the pastry is risen and golden brown. Serve the pie hot with steamed organic vegetables.

FILLETS of BRILL in RED WINE SAUCE

Forget the old maxim that red wine and fish do not go well together. The robust sauce adds colour and richness to this excellent dish.

SERVES FOUR

4 fillets of brill, about 175–200g/6–7oz
    each, skinned
150g/5oz/10 tbsp chilled butter or
    non-hydrogenated margarine, diced,
    plus extra for greasing
115g/4oz shallots, thinly sliced
200ml/7fl oz/scant 1 cup robust
    red wine
200ml/7fl oz/scant 1 cup fish stock
salt and ground white pepper
fresh chervil or flat leaf parsley leaves,
    to garnish

COOK'S TIP
If your baking dish is not flameproof,
then pour the liquid into a pan to cook
on the stove.

1 Preheat the oven to 180°C/350°F/ Gas 4. Season the fish on both sides with a little salt and plenty of pepper. Generously butter a flameproof dish, which is large enough to take all the brill fillets in a single layer without overlapping. Spread the shallots over the base and lay the fish fillets on top. Season.

2 Pour in the red wine and fish stock, cover the dish and bring the liquid to just below boiling point. Transfer the dish to the oven and bake for 6–8 minutes, or until the brill is just cooked.

3 Using a fish slice, carefully lift the fish and shallots on to a serving dish, cover with foil and keep hot.

4 Transfer the dish to the hob and bring the cooking liquid to the boil over a high heat. Cook it until it has reduced by half. Lower the heat and whisk in the chilled butter or margarine, one piece at a time, to make a smooth, shiny sauce. Season with salt and ground white pepper, set aside and keep hot.

5 Divide the shallots among four warmed plates and lay the brill fillets on top. Pour the sauce over and around the fish and garnish with the chervil or flat leaf parsley.

VARIATION
Turbot, halibut or John Dory fillets can also be cooked in this way. Make sure that your fish is caught sustainably.

SMOKED HADDOCK with MUSTARD CABBAGE

A wide range of organic mustards are available – wholegrain is used in this warming winter dish, but any type can be used instead.

SERVES FOUR

1 Savoy or pointu cabbage

675g/1½lb undyed smoked haddock fillet

300ml/½ pint/1¼ cups milk or
    soya milk

½ onion, peeled and sliced into rings

2 bay leaves

½ lemon, sliced

4 white peppercorns

4 ripe tomatoes

50g/2oz/¼ cup butter or 50ml/3½ tbsp
    olive oil

30ml/2 tbsp wholegrain mustard

juice of 1 lemon

sea salt and ground black pepper

30ml/2 tbsp chopped fresh parsley,
    to garnish

1 Cut the cabbage in half, remove the central core and thick ribs, then shred the cabbage. Cook in a pan of lightly salted boiling water, or steam over boiling water for about 10 minutes until just tender. Leave in the pan or steamer until required.

2 Meanwhile put the smoked haddock fillet in a large shallow pan with the milk, onion rings and bay leaves. Add the lemon slices and white peppercorns. Bring to simmering point, cover and poach until the fish flakes easily when tested with the tip of a sharp knife. This will take 8–10 minutes, depending on the thickness of the fillets. Take the pan off the heat and set aside until needed. Preheat the grill (broiler).

3 Cut the tomatoes in half horizontally, season them with a little salt and plenty of pepper and grill (broil) until lightly browned. Drain the cabbage, refresh under cold water and drain again.

4 Heat the butter or oil in a shallow pan or wok, add the cabbage and toss over the heat for 2 minutes. Mix in the mustard and season to taste, then add the cabbage to a warmed serving dish.

5 Drain the haddock. Skin and cut the fish into four pieces. Place on top of the cabbage with some of the cooked onion rings and grilled tomato halves. Pour on the lemon juice, then sprinkle with chopped fresh parsley and serve.

PLUM CHARLOTTES with FOAMY CALVADOS SAUCE

A variety of different types of organic plums are available in late autumn and early winter – from tangy yellow greengages to sweet and juicy Victorias.

SERVES FOUR

115g/4oz/½ cup butter or
   non-hydrogenated margarine, melted
50g/2oz/¼ cup demerara (raw) sugar
450g/1lb ripe plums, stoned (pitted) and
   thickly sliced
25g/1oz/2 tbsp unrefined caster
   (superfine) sugar
30ml/2 tbsp water
1.5ml/¼ tsp ground cinnamon
25g/1oz/¼ cup ground almonds
8–10 large slices of white or wholemeal
   (whole-wheat) bread

For the Calvados sauce
3 egg yolks
40g/1½oz/3 tbsp unrefined caster
   (superfine) sugar
30ml/2 tbsp Calvados

1 Preheat the oven to 190°C/375°F/ Gas 5. Line the base of four individual 10cm/4in-diameter deep, earthenware ramekin dishes with baking parchment. Brush evenly and thoroughly with a little of the melted butter or margarine, then sprinkle each dish with a little of the demerara sugar, rotating the dish in your hands to coat the insides evenly.

VARIATIONS
• Slices of peeled pear or eating apples can be used in this recipe instead of the stoned, sliced plums.
• If you cannot find organic Calvados any organic fruit-based spirit will work in this dish.

2 Place the stoned plum slices in a pan with the caster sugar, water and ground cinnamon and cook gently for 5 minutes, or until the plums have softened slightly. Leave the plums to cool, then stir in the ground almonds.

3 Cut the crusts off the bread and then use a plain pastry cutter to cut out four rounds to fit the bases of the ramekins. Dip the bread rounds into the melted butter and fit them into the dishes. Cut four more rounds to fit the tops of the dishes and set aside.

4 Cut the remaining bread into strips, dip into the melted butter and use to line the sides of the ramekins completely.

5 Divide the plum mixture among the lined dishes and level the tops with the back of a spoon. Place the bread rounds on top and brush with the remaining butter. Place the ramekins on a baking sheet and bake for 25 minutes.

6 Make the sauce just before the charlottes are ready. Place the egg yolks and caster sugar in a large bowl, and whisk them together until pale. Place the bowl over a pan of simmering water and whisk in the Calvados. Continue whisking until the mixture is very light and frothy.

7 Remove the charlottes from the oven and turn out on to warm serving plates. Pour a little sauce over and around the charlottes and serve immediately.

COOK'S TIP
For an extra creamy dessert, serve the puddings with Greek (US strained plain) yogurt or crème fraîche.

BAKED MAPLE and PECAN CROISSANT PUDDING

This variation of the classic English bread and butter pudding uses rich, flaky croissants, topped with a delicious mixture of organic fruit and nuts. Maple syrup-flavoured custard completes this mouthwatering dessert.

SERVES FOUR

75g/3oz/scant ½ cup sultanas
   (golden raisins)
45ml/3 tbsp brandy
4 large croissants
50g/2oz/¼ cup butter or non-hydrogenated
   margarine, plus extra for greasing
40g/1½oz/⅓ cup pecan nuts,
   roughly chopped
3 eggs, lightly beaten
300ml/½ pint/1¼ cups milk or soya milk
150ml/¼ pint/⅔ cup single (light) cream
   or soya cream
120ml/4fl oz/½ cup maple syrup
25g/1oz/2 tbsp demerara (raw) sugar
maple syrup and pouring (half-and-half)
   cream or soya cream, to serve (optional)

1 Lightly grease the base and sides of a small, shallow ovenproof dish. Place the sultanas and brandy in a small pan and heat gently, until warm. Leave to stand for 1 hour.

2 Cut the croissants into thick slices and then spread with butter on one side.

3 Arrange the croissant slices butter side uppermost and slightly overlapping in the greased dish. Sprinkle the brandy-soaked sultanas and the roughly chopped pecan nuts evenly over the buttered croissant slices.

4 In a large bowl, beat the eggs and milk together, then gradually beat in the single or soya cream and maple syrup.

COOK'S TIPS
• The main sweetener in this recipe is maple syrup. It is made by tapping the sap of the maple tree. Organic maple syrup is not overprocessed so it retains its natural richness.
• Pecan nuts are an elongated nut in a glossy red oval-shaped shell, but are usually sold shelled. They are native to the USA and have a sweet, mild flavour. Pecans are most commonly used in pecan pie but are also popular in ice creams and cakes. Walnuts can be substituted for pecans in most recipes, and they would be perfect in this one if you don't have any pecan nuts.

5 Pour the egg custard through a sieve, over the croissants, fruit and nuts in the dish. Leave the pudding to stand for 30 minutes so that some of the custard is absorbed by the croissants. Preheat the oven to 180°F/350°C/Gas 4.

6 Sprinkle the demerara sugar evenly over the top, then cover the dish with foil. Bake the pudding for 30 minutes, then remove the foil and continue to cook for about 20 minutes, or until the custard is set and the top is golden brown.

7 Leave the pudding to cool for about 15 minutes before serving warm with extra maple syrup and a little pouring cream or soya cream, if you like.

VARIATION
Thickly sliced one-day-old bread, large slices of brioche or fruit bread could be used instead of the croissants. Slightly stale one-day-old croissants are easier to slice and butter; they also soak up the custard more easily.

ORANGE MARMALADE CHOCOLATE LOAF

The cream in this recipe replaces butter to make a mouthwatering moist dark chocolate cake, finished with a bitter-sweet sticky marmalade filling and topping.

SERVES EIGHT

115g/4oz dark (bittersweet) chocolate
3 eggs
175g/6oz/scant 1 cup unrefined caster
   (superfine) sugar
175ml/6fl oz/¾ cup sour cream
200g/7oz/1¾ cups self-raising
   (self-rising) flour

For the filling and topping
200g/7oz/⅔ cup bitter orange marmalade
115g/4oz dark (bittersweet) chocolate
60ml/4 tbsp sour cream
shredded orange rind, to decorate

1 Preheat the oven to 190°C/375°F/Gas 5. Grease a 900g/2lb loaf tin (pan) lightly, then line the base with a piece of baking parchment. Break the chocolate into pieces. Melt the chocolate in a heatproof bowl placed over hot water.

2 Combine the eggs and sugar in a separate bowl. Using a hand-held electric mixer, beat the mixture until it is thick and creamy, then stir in the sour cream and melted chocolate. Fold in the flour evenly using a metal spoon.

3 Pour the mixture into the prepared tin and bake for about 1 hour, or until well risen and firm to the touch. Cool for a few minutes in the tin, then turn out onto a wire rack and let the loaf cool completely.

4 Make the filling. Spoon two-thirds of the marmalade into a small pan and melt over a low heat. Break the chocolate into pieces. Melt the chocolate in a heatproof bowl placed over hot water. Stir the chocolate into the marmalade with the sour cream.

5 Slice the cake across into three layers and sandwich back together with about half the marmalade filling. Spread the rest over the top of the cake and leave to set. Spoon the remaining marmalade over the cake and sprinkle with shredded orange rind, to decorate.

COOK'S TIP
A fantastic variety of different types of organic marmalades are available, including farmhouse and hand-made regional varieties.

ORANGE and NUT SEMOLINA CAKE

In eastern Mediterranean cooking semolina is used in many desserts. Here it provides a spongy base for soaking up a deliciously fragrant spicy syrup.

SERVES TEN

For the cake
115g/4oz/½ cup unsalted butter or non-hydrogenated margarine, softened
115g/4oz/generous ½ cup unrefined caster (superfine) sugar or rapadura
finely grated rind of 1 orange, plus 30ml/2 tbsp juice
3 eggs
175g/6oz/1 cup semolina
10ml/2 tsp baking powder
115g/4oz/1 cup ground hazelnuts
natural (plain) yogurt, to serve

To finish
350g/12oz/1¾ cups unrefined caster (superfine) sugar or rapadura
2 cinnamon sticks, halved
juice of 1 lemon
60ml/4 tbsp orange flower water
50g/2oz/½ cup unblanched hazelnuts, toasted and chopped
50g/2oz/½ cup blanched almonds, toasted and chopped
shredded rind of 1 orange, to decorate

1 Preheat the oven to 220°C/425°F/Gas 7. Grease and line the base of a deep 23cm/9in square solid-based cake tin (pan).

2 Lightly cream the butter in a large bowl. Add the sugar or rapadura, orange rind and juice, eggs, semolina, baking powder and hazelnuts and beat the ingredients together until smooth.

3 Transfer to the prepared tin and level the surface. Bake for 20–25 minutes until just firm and golden. Leave to cool in the tin.

4 To make the syrup, put the unrefined caster sugar in a small heavy pan with 550ml/18fl oz/2½ cups water and the halved cinnamon sticks. Heat gently, stirring occasionally with a wooden spoon, until the sugar has dissolved completely.

5 Bring to the boil and boil fast, without stirring, for 5 minutes. Measure half the boiling syrup and add the lemon juice and orange flower water to it. Pour over the cake. Reserve the remainder of the syrup in the pan.

6 Leave the cake in the tin until the syrup is absorbed, then turn it out on to a plate and cut diagonally into diamond-shaped portions. Sprinkle with the nuts.

7 Boil the remaining syrup until slightly thickened then pour it over the cake. Sprinkle the shredded orange rind over the cake to decorate and serve with natural yogurt.

JAMS AND PRESERVES

Preserving fruits and vegetables is one of the best ways of enjoying seasonal produce all year round. In summer and autumn, there is an abundance of sweet juicy berries, perfect for making jams and jellies to be enjoyed at any time of year. If you grow your own vegetables, then gluts offer the perfect opportunity to preserve the produce of the growing season and test some new recipes all at the same time. When produce is in season, it is at its most economical to buy, so even if you don't grow your own, farmers' markets are a great way to locate quantities of top-quality fruit and vegetables. Confit of Slow-cooked Onions, Piccalilli and Tomato Chutney with their piquant and intense flavours are ideal recipes to accompany and enliven plain cold meats. Homemade jams and preserves are a taste sensation that cannot be bettered by bought varieties, and two favourites are featured here, Orange Marmalade and Strawberry Jam.

CONFIT of SLOW-COOKED ONIONS

This jam of caramelized onions will keep for several days in a sealed jar in the refrigerator.
You can use red, white or yellow onions, but yellow onions will give the sweetest result.

2 Season with salt and plenty of pepper, then add the thyme, bay leaf and sugar. Cook slowly, uncovered, for another 15–20 minutes, or until the onions are very soft and dark.

3 Add the prunes, vinegar and wine with 60ml/4 tbsp water and cook over a low heat, stirring frequently, for a further 20 minutes, or until most of the liquid has evaporated. Add a little water and reduce the heat if the mixture dries too quickly.

4 Adjust the seasoning, adding more sugar and/or vinegar to taste. Leave the confit to cool, then stir in the remaining 5ml/1 tsp oil. The confit is best stored for 24 hours before eating. Serve either cold or warm.

VARIATION
Baby onions with tomato and orange
Gently fry 500g/1¼lb peeled pickling (pearl) onions or small *cipollini* in 60ml/ 4 tbsp olive oil until lightly browned, then sprinkle in 45ml/3 tbsp of unrefined soft light brown sugar. Let the onions caramelize a little, then add 7.5ml/ 1½ tsp crushed coriander seeds, 250ml/ 8fl oz/1 cup red wine, 2 bay leaves, a few thyme sprigs, 3 strips orange zest and 45ml/3 tbsp tomato purée (paste) and the juice of 1 orange. Cook very gently, uncovered, for 1 hour, stirring occasionally until the sauce is thick and reduced. Uncover for the last 20 minutes of cooking time. Sharpen with 15–30ml/ 1–2 tbsp sherry vinegar and serve cold, sprinkled with chopped fresh parsley.

MAKES 500G/1¼LBS

30ml/2 tbsp olive oil
15g/½oz/1 tbsp butter
500g/1¼lb onions, sliced
3–5 fresh thyme sprigs
1 fresh bay leaf
30ml/2 tbsp unrefined light muscovado
    (brown) sugar, plus a little extra
50g/2oz/¼ cup prunes, chopped
30ml/2 tbsp balsamic vinegar,
    plus a little extra
120ml/4fl oz/½ cup red wine
sea salt and ground black pepper

1 Reserve 5ml/1 tsp of the oil, then heat the rest with the butter in a small, heavy pan. Add the onions, cover and cook gently for 15 minutes, stirring occasionally.

PICCALILLI

Undoubtedly one of the most popular relishes, piccalilli can be eaten with grilled
sausages, ham or chops, cold meats or a strong, well-flavoured cheese such as Cheddar.

MAKES 1.8KG/4LB

1 large cauliflower, cut into small florets
450g/1lb pickling (pearl) onions, peeled
   and quartered
900g/2lb mixed vegetables, such as marrow
   (large zucchini), cucumber, French
   (green) beans
225g/8oz/1 cup salt
2.4 litres/4 pints/10 cups cold water
200g/7oz/1 cup granulated (white) sugar
2 garlic cloves, peeled and crushed
10ml/2 tsp mustard powder
5ml/1 tsp ground ginger
1 litre/1³/4 pints/4 cups distilled
   (white) vinegar
25g/1oz/¹/4 cup plain (all-purpose) flour
15ml/1 tbsp turmeric

1 To prepare the vegetables, seed and finely dice the marrow and cucumber. Top and tail the French beans, then cut them into 2.5cm/1 in lengths.

2 Layer the vegetables in a large (not plastic) bowl, generously sprinkling each layer with salt. Pour over the water, cover the bowl with clear film (plastic wrap) and leave to soak for 24 hours.

3 Drain the soaked vegetables, and discard the brine. Rinse well in several changes of cold water to remove as much salt as possible, then thoroughly drain the vegetables.

COOK'S TIP
Store opened jars of piccalilli in the refrigerator.

4 Put the sugar, garlic, mustard, ginger and 900ml/1¹/2 pints/3³/4 cups vinegar in a preserving pan. Heat gently, stirring occasionally, until the sugar dissolves.

5 Add the vegetables to the pan, bring to the boil, reduce the heat and simmer for 10–15 minutes, or until the vegetables are almost tender.

6 Mix the flour and turmeric with the remaining vinegar and stir into the vegetables. Bring to the boil, stirring, and simmer for 5 minutes until thick.

7 Spoon into warmed sterilized jars, cover and seal. Store in a cool, dark place for at least 2 weeks. Use within 1 year.

TOMATO CHUTNEY

This spicy, sweet-sour chutney is delicious served with a selection of well-flavoured cheeses and crackers or bread, or with cold roast meats such as ham or turkey.

MAKES ABOUT 1.8KG/4LB

900g/2lb tomatoes, skinned
225g/8oz/1½ cups raisins
225g/8oz onions, chopped
225g/8oz/generous 1 cup caster
    (superfine) sugar
600ml/1 pint/2½ cups malt vinegar

VARIATION
Dried dates may be used in place of the raisins, and red wine or sherry vinegar may be used in place of the malt vinegar. Stone (pit) and chop the dates, or buy stoned cooking dates that have been compressed in a block and chop them finely.

1 Chop the tomatoes roughly and place in a preserving pan. Add the raisins, onions and caster sugar.

2 Pour the vinegar into the pan and bring to the boil. Simmer for 2 hours, uncovered, until soft and thickened.

3 Transfer the chutney to warmed sterilized jars. Top with waxed paper discs and lids. Store in a cool, dark place and leave to mature for 1 month. The chutney will keep unopened for up to 1 year. Once opened, store the jars in the refrigerator and use within 3 weeks.

MANGO CHUTNEY

This classic chutney is conventionally served with curries and poppadoms, but it is also delicious with baked ham or a traditional cheese ploughman's lunch.

MAKES 450G/1LB

3 firm mangoes
150ml/¼ pint/⅔ cup cider vinegar
130g/4½ oz/⅔ cup light muscovado
   (brown) sugar
1 small red chilli or jalapeño
   chilli, split
2.5cm/1in piece of fresh root ginger,
   peeled and finely chopped
1 garlic clove, finely chopped
5 cardamom pods, bruised
2.5ml/½ tsp coriander seeds, crushed
1 bay leaf
2.5ml/½ tsp salt

1 Peel the mangoes and cut the flesh off the stone (pit). Slice the mangoes lengthways, then cut across into small chunks. Place the mango in a large pan, add the vinegar and cover. Cook over a low heat for 10 minutes.

2 Stir in the muscovado sugar, chilli, ginger, garlic, cardamoms and coriander. Add the bay leaf and salt. Bring to the boil slowly, stirring often.

3 Lower the heat and simmer, uncovered, for 30 minutes or until the mixture is thick and syrupy.

4 Ladle into hot sterilized jars, seal and label. Store for 1 week before eating. Keep chilled after opening.

COOK'S TIPS
• Always use fresh fruit and avoid overripe fruit.
• Wine vinegar and cider vinegar are good for preserving colourful or light-coloured fruit and vegetables because they will not spoil the colour.
• The choice of sugar will affect the end result: light muscovado gives the richest flavour and colour; demerara (raw) sugar and golden granulated sugar give a caramel flavour; and white sugar helps to retain the colour of light ingredients.
• Never cover the pan when making chutney. Cooking the preserve uncovered allows the liquid to evaporate and the chutney to thicken. Stir well to prevent the contents from burning.

ORANGE MARMALADE

This recipes uses Seville oranges, which have a short season. It can be made as a plain
jelly marmalade, or a few fine shreds of peel can be added before putting into pots.

MAKES ABOUT 2KG/4½LB

450g/1lb Seville (Temple) oranges, washed
    (or scrubbed if they have waxy skins),
    and dried
1.75 litres /3 pints/7½ cups water
1.3kg/3lb/generous 6¾ cups preserving
    or granulated (white) sugar
60ml/4 tbsp lemon juice

1 Thinly pare and finely shred the rind
from 2 or 3 oranges. Place the shreds in
a square of muslin (cheesecloth) and tie
it into a neat bag.

2 Halve all the oranges. Squeeze out the
juice and pips (seeds), then pour the juice
and pips into a large preserving pan.

3 Roughly chop the remaining orange
peel, including all the pith, and add it to
the pan. Add the bag of shredded rind, if
using, and pour over the water. Cover
the pan with the lid and leave to soak
for at least 4 hours or overnight to
soften the fruit.

4 Bring the mixture to the boil, then
reduce the heat and simmer gently for
1½ hours. Remove the bag of rind and
check that it is tender. Simmer for
another 15–20 minutes if not. Set the
bag of rind aside.

5 Line a sieve with a double layer of
muslin and place over a large bowl. Pour
boiling water through the muslin-lined
sieve to scald the muslin. Discard the
water. Pour the peel and juices into
the sieve and leave to drain for at
least 1 hour.

6 Pour the juices into a clean pan. Add
the sugar, lemon juice and shredded
orange rind, if using. Stir over a low heat
until the sugar has dissolved, then boil
rapidly for about 10 minutes until setting
point (105°C/220°F) is reached.

7 Remove any scum from the surface.
Leave to cool until a thin skin starts to
form on the surface. Stir, then pot, cover
and seal.

COOK'S TIP
If the fruit rind contains a lot of pith, put
only a small amount in the muslin bag.

BLUEBERRY AND LIME JAM

The subtle yet fragrant flavour of blueberries can be elusive on its own. Adding a generous quantity of tangy lime juice enhances it and gives this preserve a zesty taste.

MAKES 1.3KG/3LB

1.3kg/3lb/12 cups blueberries
finely pared rind and juice of 4 limes
1kg/2¼lb/5 cups preserving sugar
  with pectin

1 Put the blueberries, lime juice and half the sugar in a large, non-metallic bowl and lightly crush the berries using a potato masher. Set aside for about 4 hours.

2 Pour the crushed berry mixture into a pan and stir in the finely pared lime rind and the remaining preserving sugar. Heat slowly, stirring continuously, until the sugar has completely dissolved.

3 Increase the heat and bring to the boil. Boil rapidly for about 4 minutes, or until the jam reaches setting point (105°C/220°F).

4 Remove the pan from the heat and set aside for 5 minutes. Stir the jam gently, then pour into warmed sterilized jars. Seal the jars, then label when completely cool. Store in a cool, dark place.

COOK'S TIPS
• Blueberries are not naturally high in pectin, so extra pectin is needed for a good set.
• Warm the sugar in a low oven for about 10 minutes before adding it to the fruit. This will help it to dissolve.
• Always use the freshest fruit possible and avoid overripe fruit.
• If you wash the fruit, dry it well and use promptly because it will deteriorate on standing.
• Cook the fruit very slowly at first over a low heat to extract the maximum amount of juice and pectin. Stir the fruit frequently until very tender, but do not overcook. (Fruit skins toughen once sugar is added.)
• Stir the preserve to ensure the sugar is completely dissolved before boiling.
• Do not stir frequently when boiling. This lowers the temperature and delays reaching setting point.
• Do not move freshly potted preserves until they are cool and have set properly.
• It is wasteful to remove scum too often. To help prevent scum from forming, add a small amount of unsalted butter (about 15g/½oz/1 tbsp for every 450g/1lb of fruit) when you add the sugar. Scum does not detract from the taste of the jam but may affect its keeping qualities.

STRAWBERRY JAM

Perfectly ripe strawberries, shiny and deep red in colour, are the main ingredient of this very popular preserve. It tastes even better if the strawberries are grown organically.

MAKES 1.3KG/3LB

1kg/2¼lb/9 cups strawberries, hulled
900g/2lb/4½ cups preserving sugar
juice of 2 lemons

1 Layer the hulled strawberries with the sugar in a large bowl. Cover with clear film (plastic wrap) and leave overnight.

2 Put the strawberries into a large heavy pan. Add the lemon juice. Gradually bring to the boil, over a low heat, stirring until the sugar has dissolved.

3 Boil steadily for 10–15 minutes, or until the jam reaches setting point (see column, right). When it is ready, cool for 10 minutes in the pan.

4 Pour into warm sterilized jars, filling them right to the top. Cover and seal while the jam is still hot and label when the jars are cold.

5 Store in a cool dark place for up to one year.

SETTING POINT

The point at which jam sets is 105°C/220°F. If you don't have a sugar thermometer, put 10ml/2 tsp of the jam on to a chilled saucer. Chill for 3 minutes, then push the jam gently with your finger; if wrinkles form it is ready. If not, continue boiling, but keep checking regularly.

BRAMBLE JELLY

This jelly has an excellent intense, fruity flavour. Make sure you include large juicy berries as well as a few red unripe berries in the pan for a good fruit set.

MAKES 900G/2LB

900g/2lb/8 cups blackberries
juice of 1 lemon
about 900g/2lb/4½ cups caster
   (superfine) sugar

1 Put the fruit, 300ml/½ pint/1¼ cups water and the lemon juice in a large, heavy pan.

2 Cover and cook for 15–30 minutes or until the blackberries are very soft.

3 Ladle into a jelly bag or large sieve (strainer) lined with muslin and set over a large bowl. Leave to strain overnight. Use a large wooden spoon to mash the fruit to extract the juice further.

4 Discard the pulp. Measure the exuded juice and allow 450g/1lb sugar to every 600ml/1 pint/2½ cups fruit juice.

5 Place the sugar and liquid in a large, heavy pan and bring slowly to the boil, stirring all the time until the sugar has dissolved.

VARIATION
Redcurrant jelly is made in the same way. Reduce the sugar to 350g/12oz/1½ cups for 600ml/1 pint/2½ cups juice.

6 Boil rapidly until the jelly registers 105°C/220°F on a sugar thermometer, or test for setting by spooning a small amount on to a chilled saucer. Chill for 3 minutes, then push the mixture with your finger; if wrinkles form on the surface, it is ready. Cool for 10 minutes.

7 Skim off any scum and pour the jelly into warm sterilized jars. Cover and seal while the jelly is still hot. Label when the jars are cold. Store for up to 6 months in a cool, dry place.

MINCEMEAT

This fruity mincemeat is traditionally used to fill little pies at Christmas, but it is great at any time. Try it as a filling for large tarts served with custard.

MAKES 1.8KG/4LB

500g/1¼lb tart cooking apples, peeled, cored and finely diced
115g/4oz/½ cup ready-to-eat dried apricots, coarsely chopped
900g/2lb/5⅓ cups luxury dried mixed fruit
115g/4oz/1 cup whole blanched almonds, chopped
175g/6oz/1 cup shredded beef or vegetarian suet (chilled, grated shortening)
225g/8oz/generous 1 cup dark muscovado (molasses) sugar
grated rind and juice of 1 orange
grated rind and juice of 1 lemon
5ml/1 tsp ground cinnamon
2.5ml/½ tsp grated nutmeg
2.5ml/½ tsp ground ginger
120ml/4fl oz/½ cup brandy

3 Spoon the mincemeat into cool sterilized jars, pressing down well, and being careful not to trap any air bubbles. Cover and seal.

4 Store the jars in a cool, dark place for at least 4 weeks before using. Once opened, store in the refrigerator and use within 4 weeks. Unopened, the mincemeat will keep for 1 year.

BOTTLING PREPARATION
Wash and dry glass jars in hot soapy water, ensuring that they do not carry any scent of the original content, if you are reusing jars. If they do, fill the jars with a solution of 5ml/1 tsp bicarbonate of soda and hot water. Allow to stand for a few minutes. Wash thoroughly. Set the oven temperature to 110°C/225°F/Gas ¼ and place the glass jars in the oven 30 minutes before you are ready to bottle the produce. Allow the jars to heat up for 10 minutes, then set them aside on a heatproof board. Allow to cool slightly for ease of handling, then fill the jars to the top, ensuring there are no air pockets in which mould may grow. Place a disc of waxed paper over the top of the produce and seal with the lid. Remember to add a label naming the contents and the date of making. Store as directed.

1 Put the apples, apricots, dried fruit, almonds, suet and sugar in a large non-metallic bowl and stir together until thoroughly combined.

2 Add the orange and lemon rind and juice, cinnamon, nutmeg, ginger and brandy and mix well. Cover the bowl with a clean dish towel and leave to stand in a cool place for 2 days, stirring occasionally.

COOK'S TIP
If, when opened, the mincemeat seems dry, pour a little extra brandy or orange juice into the jar and gently stir in. You may need to remove a spoonful or two of the mincemeat from the jar to do this.

INDEX